# CHAOTIC ELECTIONS!

## A Mathematician Looks at Voting

# CHAOTIC ELECTIONS!

## A Mathematician Looks at Voting

### Donald G. Saari

AMERICAN MATHEMATICAL SOCIETY

2000 *Mathematics Subject Classification*. Primary 91B12, 91B14, 00A05.

Cover illustration courtesy of Loel Barr.

---

**Library of Congress Cataloging-in-Publication Data**

Saari, D. (Donald)
    Chaotic elections! : a mathematician looks at voting / Donald G. Saari.
        p. cm.
    Includes bibliographical references and index.
    ISBN 0-8218-2847-9 (alk. paper)
    1. Voting.    I. Title.

JF1001 .S227    2001
324.9—dc21                                                                 2001022386

---

∞ The paper used in this book is acid-free and falls within the guidelines
established to ensure permanence and durability.
Visit the AMS home page at URL: http://www.ams.org/

10 9 8 7 6 5 4 3 2 1      06 05 04 03 02 01

Dedicated to four adventurous delights who have a deep curiosity about everything!

## Heili, Mikko, Torik, and Tyler

Who knows; should we ever adopt a reasonable election procedure, some day one of them be may become President.

# Contents

# Preface

It is reasonable to treat this book as a personal aftershock which manifests the collision of two events. The first was a public event; it was the 2000 U.S. Presidential election. Everyone knows who was legally declared the President. But who *really* won? While each of us probably has a strong opinion, let's face it; nobody will ever know.

The second "colliding" event was a personal one; in January 2000 I published some papers ([**56, 57**]) which finally resolved to my satisfaction (well, at least for now) a two-centuries-old mathematical problem concerning the source and explanation of the paradoxes and problems of voting procedures. The resolution of this problem, which was initiated in the French Academy of Sciences by the mathematicians Jean Charles de Borda, Marie-Jean-Antoine-Nicolas de Caritat Condorcet, Pierre-Simon Laplace, and others near the end of the 1700s, attracted brief popular-press attention. As such it was easy for reporters to learn about my research if a contested election would ever arise.

Such an election surely did occur! The effect of the two forces colliding prompted several reporters to question whether mathematics could explain the election debate about Florida. To be honest, I don't think anyone other than those delightful characters in Lewis Carroll's "Alice in Wonderland" could fully explain what happened in Florida. On the other hand, mathematics does provide answers and guidance about what should be done in the future. It is worth enlisting the power of mathematics to shed new light on these issues which are of particularly crucial public interest.

The purpose of the book is to explain what can go wrong in elections and why. The first part of each chapter is directed toward a general reader with patience and a willingness to wade through some minimal mathematical notation. My advice to the reader is that when a chapter seems to getting a little heavy, read a bit more. If it becomes too heavy, as measured by a growing urge to relegate the book to a dusty pile of "future good intentions" or the waste basket, then just jump ahead to the next chapter. The reason for this advice is based on the structure of the book; the last part of each chapter is intended to give a reader who is a bit more mathematically sophisticated some insight into why the results are true.

Let me emphasize that this is *not* a research monograph; while professionals in this area may discover several new results, the book is *not* directed toward them. Instead, my intention is to provide a more readable exposition of my recent research results so that the reader can better appreciate what can happen in elections. I expect you will be surprised. Hopefully, these notions are described in a way so that the reader can develop an understanding of what can happen without being hindered by highly technical details. (Actual proofs are left for the original papers, or, maybe, a future, technical monograph.) Indeed, I hope that some readers become sufficiently disturbed about the dangers of our current voting procedure that they become activists in demanding a change.

Another goal of mine is to attract mathematicians to the growing and fascinating area of the mathematics of the social sciences. As some mathematicians may shy away only because of a lack of training about these topics, it may be instructive to briefly outline how I got interested and started in this area. After all, the mathematics of voting is not a research topic normally studied and represented in a mathematics department. Furthermore, as is true of most mathematicians, my training and earlier research interests are very far removed from this area; they emphasized techniques from analysis and dynamical systems and, in particular, questions about the Newtonian $n$-body problem. These bodies move, they don't vote.

Part of what attracted me came from being a mathematician. A particular delight and privilege of being a mathematician is that our training permits us to investigate and examine so many diverse aspects of our surrounding existence. Indeed, there are many other topics out there just waiting — almost begging — for a mathematical analysis to remove the mystery and provide guidance. Let me encourage mathematicians to investigate some of them. You have my promise; with patience and imagination, these studies can be fascinating!

As for my story, I can just say, "Beware of hobbies!" There I was, happily examining the evolution of Newton's universe, the effects of colliding particles in gravitational systems, and other dynamical effects when, almost as a hobby, I discovered voting problems.

It is not important to explain what initially attracted me; it happened. Instead, let me warn you; like an addictive drug, once you start fooling around in this area, it becomes difficult to quit. As is probably true of others, I expected to exercise superb discipline. At first, it was only on weekends — and strictly for recreational purposes — that I would experiment with small doses of election paradoxes. I knew I could handle it. I thought I had the willpower to just recreationally experience these issues and then return to the $n$-body problem the next morning. Very quickly, however, I was caught up with a personal compulsion to consume more and more of the mathematics of elections — the need extended even to evenings during the week. And then, well, I discovered that my dependency for a research fix in this area would start already most mornings, and it would continue through the day. I was hooked.

Without question, this area provides incredible temptations for any mathematician. To partially explain, when I first discovered this area, it was accepted that election procedures could cause paradoxical problems. But, somewhat surprisingly, only a few paradoxical examples were actually known and available. Be honest; if presented with this kind of intriguing but limited information, any mathematician would want to know whether this is the full story. Are these limited number of examples concocted, or are they real? Are there more? How many more? What are they? Can we find all of them? How likely are they? How about in actual elections; do we need to worry about these paradoxes?

The difficulty is that, unlike some politicians, a tempted mathematician almost always inhales the intellectual challenge. Almost by training, a mathematician needs to know, for instance, whether it is possible to characterize everything that can occur. In other words, a first, irresistible challenge for a mathematician is to determine and list *all possible election "paradoxes."*

To appreciate the temptation of this challenge, remember that a "paradox" is an unexpected, unexplained behavior. Thus, the challenge facing a mathematician is to discover and then catalogue *all possible election oddities that we do not expect to occur.* Can you think of a more enticing temptation to dangle before a mathematician? No wonder I partially dropped off the Newtonian $n$-body wagon.

But how does one discover everything that we don't expect to exist? When faced with a new difficulty, we tend to revert to those tools with which we are most comfortable. For me, coming from the dynamics of mathematical astronomy, these are the tools of "symbolic" or "chaotic dynamics." To see the relevance, remember that a particularly important success of this area of dynamical systems is how it allowed us to discover and even catalogue dynamical behavior that nobody expected to occur. The technical difficulty in applying this material to voting, however, is that tallying ballots does not involve dynamics with horseshoes and homoclinic points.

However, in a manner described at the end of Chapter 3, rather than the actual chaotic dynamics, concepts which are central to this area of "unexpected mathematical behavior" can be modified to identify all possible "election paradoxes" which could occur with any number of candidates, with any number of voters, and with any of the standard, basic, voting procedures. As described in Chapters 2 and 3, the conclusions are distinctly discouraging for any democracy. Although my later research uncovered other mathematical approaches which more efficiently explain these difficulties in a much sharper manner, the notions coming from chaotic dynamics continue to be the most illustrative to explain what happens and why.

Every so often, one finds one of those philosophical articles marveling about the "Unreasonable effectiveness of mathematics." While it is not appropriate for me to suddenly become a philosopher, let me remind the reader that these articles often mention how the abstract power of mathematics allows conclusions to be transferred from one research area to another.

Voting is no exception; the results described in this book can be extended in unexpected ways to other research topics. It turns out, for instance, that the discouraging assertions about voting methods extend to describe unexpected troubling conclusions about most aggregation procedures. After all, voting is just an aggregation method designed to assemble considerable amounts of data — the voters' preferences — into the simpler, digestible form of the election ranking. The same goal characterizes the fields of statistics, probability, game theory, economics, and most of the social sciences. I provide a taste of these connections in Chapter 6.

Another interesting connection between dynamics and voting is that many of the concepts which occur in chaotic dynamics have a parallel property with voting theory. For instance, one of the better known aspects of "chaos" is that familiar phrase "sensitivity with respect to initial conditions." This comment means that even a miniscule change in the starting position for the dynamics can have a huge effect. Eventually, this small starting change can result in a drastically different future for the dynamics. In voting theory, the parallel is where a slight change in how the voters mark their ballots — even if only one voter does so — can cause a surprising change in the outcome. For voting theory, one parallel aspect of this behavior is associated with "strategic" or "manipulative behavior"; this topic is discussed in Chapter 4.

To continue with how "dynamics" has influenced the development of "voting theory," recall how when "chaotic dynamics" became a widely discussed topic, it forced mathematicians to make a choice. They could throw up their collective hands in despair and then quit because the motion seems to be random where nothing is predictable, or they could dismiss this negative attitude by trying to uncover the underlying structure of the dynamics. Probably because of their eternal optimism and pragmatism, mathematicians did the latter.

Similarly, it is counterproductive to stop with dismay once we have identified and classified the many different kinds of allowable election paradoxes. Instead, the next step is to understand why they occur, how often, and whether it is possible to find some relief. As explained in Chapter 5, this search for relief is accomplished by using "symmetry" as a tool to determine what it is that the voters really want.

This is not the end of connections with chaos. In Chapter 6, I describe a mathematical problem that has had interesting ramifications in the United States. It is the source of the first Presidential veto; it is the reason we have 435 seats in the House of Representatives. While several attempts have been made to resolve this difficulty, corrective effects turn out to be much like trying to push an inflated balloon into a small package; push here and a new problem jumps out elsewhere. As indicated, the source of the difficulties is "chaos"; this time, the description is based on the true dynamical effect.

I want to end by thanking several people. My thanks to John Ewing, Executive Director of the American Mathematical Society, and Sergei Gelfand, who is in charge of the AMS book program, for contacting me and strongly encouraging me to write this book. My warm thanks and appreciation to everyone in the AMS book production division for their rapid, efficient, and helpful production of this book; thanks to them, this publishing experience was enjoyable! Much of this research was done while in the mathematics department at Northwestern University; this was my delightful academic home for many (I won't say how many) years, so my deep thanks go to this institution. My thanks also go to Arthur and Hap Pancoe who endowed my Northwestern University "Pancoe Chair" under which much of this research was done, and then for our subsequent friendship and their interests in my research pursuits.

My new academic home, the University of California, Irvine, has been most accommodating; my thanks to all here and, in particular, to Duncan Luce who has been so helpful! My thanks for NSF support of this research; my thanks to George Hazelrigg for his continued interest in these issues. My thanks to Katri Sieberg who read and critiqued portions of the original manuscript. As always, my deepest thanks go to my wife, Lillian Saari, who went beyond reading and critiquing the manuscript to help research some of the described events.

February 2001

Irvine, California

# Chapter 1

# A Mess of an Election

What an amazing, pragmatic civics lesson! While election day occasionally offers suspense, usually it provides only a minor deviation from our standard routine. We drive to the polls and vote, gossip with colleagues at work about who might win, return home for dinner, and briefly turn on the TV to find the projected election outcomes, outcomes which may be predicted within minutes after the close of the polls and even before many ballot boxes are even opened. In fact, with rapid media predictions removing much of the election eve suspense, some of us might share a perverse wish for a close election if only to prolong the interest. As the November 2000 U.S. Presidential election proved, "Beware of what you wish; it might come true."

The 2000 U.S. Presidential election taught us several important lessons. It taught us that ballots cast need not be ballots counted; that voting machines may provide a rapid count, but not necessarily a full and accurate one. It expanded our vocabulary to include chads, dangling chads, pregnant chads, and dimpled ballots — all terms used to describe why certain ballots may, or may not, have been counted in the Presidential tally in the state of Florida. We learned the value of emphasizing patience and accuracy over speed in making statistical projections; all major television networks were acutely embarrassed on election night by forecasting a Florida victory for Vice President Al Gore, then withdrawing that premature prediction, next predicting that Governor George W. Bush would win, and finally retracting even that forecast. More than a month later, the outcome remained in doubt.

We learned the value of voting when an extra vote per Florida precinct, or maybe even a couple more forceful punches of the ballots per precinct, might have determined already on election night, one way or the other, the next U.S. President. We were reminded about the gullibility of voters when, five days before the election, the Florida attorney general declared that the normal election day was for all voters "regardless of party affiliation." Her unusual statement was to educate those voters who believed a widely circulated joke email message "announcing" that, because of the expected high voter turnout, Republicans were to vote on the normal election day and Democrats the day after. We observed an election which, by any statistical standard, was an absolute draw; no matter what the courts, legislators, recounts, and lawyers may argue, it will remain too close to call.

Some citizens may even have discovered that the U.S. Electoral College is an institution without faculty, fraternities, or even a football team. Instead, it is a Constitutional relic reflecting a less democratic time — a time when trust in selecting the country's leaders was not placed with the citizens, but delegated to state legislatures who selected the electors. We may have been alarmed when reminded by Justice Scalia of the U.S. Supreme Court, and then by a majority of the court in its historical December 12, 2000, decision, that there is no wording in the Constitution guaranteeing the right for American voters to vote for the President — either indirectly for electors of the Electoral College or directly. This court decision effectively awarded the presidency to Mr. Bush.

The only guarantees which did emerge from this election were disturbing. Court actions, political maneuvering, and even the highly public, conflicting views by Supreme Court Justices Stevens and Scalia about whether or not public confidence would erode with a continued recount of Florida votes (i.e., if Mr. Gore were ahead in the polls when the court ruled in favor of Mr. Bush, then the voters might not view Bush's victory with any legitimacy) ensured that whoever would be elected, many voters would believe that the President assumed his position illegitimately. Indeed, a Los Angeles Times survey[1] showed that 44% of the voters thought Gore would have won the Presidency if a recount had been permitted while only 33% of them thought Bush would have been victorious. This sentiment was later echoed by President Clinton when, less than two weeks before Bush's inauguration, he remarked to a partisan Chicago gathering, "The only way they could win the election was to stop the voting in Florida." The L.A. Times further reported that over a third of the surveyed voters had some doubt about the legitimacy of Bush's victory. What a mess!

Are these the real lessons? They may be for the short term. But, for a longer term and from the perspective of a mathematician, the answer must be a loud and emphatic *NO!* Instead, there are far more fundamental, important, but subtle causes of the chaotic election mess. After introducing

---

[1]Sunday, December 17, 2000.

some of them in an intuitive manner in this introductory chapter, I will explore them more carefully in later chapters.

Incidentally, in the light of the chaotic 2000 election, it is both amusing and appropriate that some of the mathematics needed to understand election methods involves "chaos." (All concepts needed for this discussion are introduced.) Well, more precisely, it involves mathematical notions which come from chaos. This random appearing behavior is then countered by soothing symmetry arguments which are used to find possible resolutions.

### The real problems

Since election day, the public has been treated to an array of proposed ways to correct our elections. Some are interesting, and each might correct some form of abuse. But, quite frankly, most of these suggestions have absolutely nothing to do with the real difficulties of the Presidential election.

The real problem concerns our archaic election procedures. As it will be shown, by almost any objective measure, our standard tools of democracy are seriously flawed. They need not deliver as promised. The problem is so severe that even in settings not hindered by the complications of an Electoral College, even those election which are free from controversy, election outcomes need not mean what we commonly think they do. The bothersome reality is that our election outcomes can fail to reflect the wishes of the voters.

This electoral difficulty is not restricted to the historical Presidential election of November 2000; it is a recurring problem that stands ready to plague all of our elections on an uncomfortably regular basis. As a challenge that I briefly discuss later, explain what happened in 1998 when, with only about 37% of the vote, Jesse Ventura beat Hubert Humphrey and Norm Coleman to become the governor of the state of Minnesota. Did Ventura's victory reflect, as many of the political pundits at that time claimed, that this election manifested a revolt among the voters? Did it, as others argued, reflect the views of the many young, first-time voters attracted to the polls by the charisma of Ventura? Or, is there a simpler, more accurate, and basic mathematical explanation?

The point which will be made is that our basic voting procedures can generate problems so worrisome that it is reasonable to worry about the legitimacy of most election outcomes. This is not a conjecture; mathematical support will be provided.

What elections should we worry about? Quite frankly, any which involves three or more candidates and where the winning candidate fails to receive a majority vote. This means we should wonder about the outcomes for our governor, or senator, or mayor, or even the local coroner. In social groups or academic departments, we should question whether the elected chair, or budget committee, or applicant hired for that one tenure-track position represents whom the voters really wanted. Even more, we should wonder what does the phrase "whom the voters really want" mean.

Election outcomes can significantly influence our lifes. Consequently, if subtle and hidden mathematical structures can cause doubt about election outcomes, then something must be done. As I will argue, this concern of finding election alternatives and options is sufficiently subtle and important that it needs the attention and help of mathematics and mathematicians.

## 1. Electoral College

To start, it is worth addressing the common cry, supported by many including U.S. Senator Hillary Clinton (D-NY) right after she was elected in the 2000 elections, that the U.S. Electoral College must go. This is not a new issue; there have been hundreds of attempts to rid the American scene of a procedure viewed by many as being archaic.

The National Board of the influential League of Women Voters has consistently stated their belief "that the direct-popular-vote method for electing the President and Vice-President is essential to representative government. The League of Women Voters believes, therefore, that the electoral college should be abolished." The LWV is not alone; labor as represented by the AFL-CIO and the UAW, business organizations such as the U.S. Chamber of Commerce, the National Federation of Independent Business, and other influential groups such as the American Bar Association and the NAACP have expressed similar sentiments. Just days before the 2000 election, U.S. Senator R. Durbin (D-Illinois) introduced a resolution calling for the direct election (with a runoff) of the President and Vice President.

What an absolute waste of time and effort. Realistically, even if such action is desired by most people, this change never will happen. Let me explain why.

The story starts with Justice Scalia's reminder that American voters do not have a Constitutional right to vote for the President. This is because the framers of the Constitution envisioned an elitist approach where the states would select responsible representatives to meet and determine the next President and Vice President. However, times and attitudes changed. Today all states have Presidential elections.

While political philosophy and practice have changed, the Constitutional Article II clause has not. Consequently, rather than voting directly for a Presidential candidate, the American voter votes for their state's *electors*;

the electors still make the actual decision.[2] They do so on a December day specified by the U.S. Constitution when the 538 electors assemble at their respective state capitals to vote for the President and Vice President of the United States.

Why 538 electors? This number reflects a political attempt to avoid a fascinating mathematical paradox, a paradox which is described in Chapter 6. Incidentally, this mathematical phenomenon not only explains the reason for several historical events, but it continues to plague the United States and the elections in many other countries. Indeed, it is safe to predict that within the next couple of decades this mathematical construct will generate disputes sufficiently severe to require the attention of the Supreme Court.

For now, accept that each state receives an elector for each of its members in the House of Representatives and in the Senate. There are 435 congressional representatives and 100 senators, leading to 535 electors. The last three electors represent the District of Columbia. Since the election decision is determined by the electors, it is easy to imagine a scenario where the elected President could be the loser in the popular vote. This is not speculation; it happened with John Quincy Adams in 1824, with Rutherford Hayes in 1876, with Benjamin Harrison in 1888, and most recently with George W. Bush in 2000.[3]

**1.1. Political power.** The only way to eliminate the Electoral College is with a Constitutional amendment. For passage, the amendment must be ratified by two-thirds of the House and of the Senate. While such a vote may be possible, the real hurdle is that the amendment must also be ratified by three-fourths of the states. This state support is extremely unlikely to ever materialize if only for the simple but pragmatic reason of "political power," or maybe to ensure a small state's comfortable survival.

To explain, consider an extreme setting where the hypothetical state of "Superior" has precisely six voters. What candidate would bother campaigning here? Probably all of them, and actively. After all, the attracting factor is Superior's three *electoral votes*; it is not the negligible popular vote.

Evidence that this is a real phenomenon can be found in any Presidential election. With a strictly popular vote, for instance, no candidate would bother campaigning in the delightful but small, remote, and often frigid city of Green Bay, Wisconsin. Yet, the 2000 Presidential search for the closely

---

[2] Although some states have laws requiring the electors to vote according to the state's popular vote, in reality, the electors can vote in any way they desire. In the 2000 election, for instance, one of Gore's electors refused to vote in her attempt to convey a political message.

[3] Adams received 31% while Andrew Jackson received 41%. Hayes received 48% while Samuel Tilden received 51%. Harrison received 47.8% while Grover Cleveland received 48.1%, and Gore received about 540,000 more votes than Bush out of the over 100 million cast.

contested[4] Wisconsin electoral votes had candidates and their surrogates braving the cold while standing outside in shirt sleeves in their search for popular votes from the northern part of the state. Contrast this setting with the likely scenario associated with a popular vote. Here, the election emphasis would rapidly move away from small cities and rural areas to concentrate on the large population districts such as the belts from San Francisco to San Diego, from Milwaukee to Detroit, and from Boston to Washington D.C.

The "political power" calculus of small states is not restricted to election year attention; it extends to include all of those legislative goodies handed out by congressional legislation and Presidential decree each year. After all, with the "next" Presidential campaign seemingly starting right after the conclusion of a current one,[5] each party tries to attract votes by providing for voter needs. With a popular vote, attention would focus primarily on population centers; who would care about Superior when it provides no serious popular vote return? Why care about the rural areas?

Using real states, if there were no electoral vote, then why should a candidate worry or care much about Vermont, or North or South Dakota? The wisdom reflected by the "small state–large state" compromise forged in the design of the U.S. Constitution, as manifested by there being two houses of Congress and by the Electoral College, remains in effect. For these reasons, the states with smaller populations (with 3, 4, or 5 electoral votes according to the 2000 census) — Alaska, Delaware, Hawaii, Idaho, Maine, Montana, Nebraska, Nevada, New Hampshire, New Mexico, North Dakota, Rhode Island, South Dakota, Utah, Vermont, West Virginia, and Wyoming — would be silly to support such a change. These 17 states are more than enough to sabotage passage of such a Constitutional amendment.

Even larger states, such as Colorado with its eight electors (nine after the 2000 census), would be well advised to support the Electoral College. This is the opinion of the year 2000 Colorado elector Mary Hergert who confessed that she originally opposed this archaic method — until she recognized its impact on her state. "It's really been an educational experience for us all. ... What you find is that [the Electoral College] really gives power to the small states, like Colorado. I don't think we need to change."[6] She is correct about the enhanced power. In fact after the 2000 reapportionment, there are

---

[4]Gore won Wisconsin's eleven electoral votes with only about 5500 more popular votes than Bush out of the more than two and a half million votes cast.

[5]Less than one week after the Presidential inauguration of George W. Bush, Joseph Lieberman, Gore's running mate in the 2000 election, was exploring setting up a committee to provide funds so that he could campaign across the country and create needed exposure for the 2004 presidential elections. Lieberman was not alone; already polls were being taken and other potential candidates were traveling to key states.

[6]L.A. Times, 12/19/00, p. A22.

29 states with a single digit number of electors; it is in their best interest to do whatever they can to sabotage such a "reform." Forget trying to eliminate the Electoral College; look elsewhere for change.[7]

**1.2. Measuring power.** Before searching elsewhere for political reform, it is worth using mathematics to measure the actual levels of power within the Electoral College; the conclusions are somewhat surprising and counter-intuitive. Let me start by dramatically illustrating the traditional "number counting" argument in terms of the hypothetical state of Superior.

For Superior, two of the six voters are U.S. Senators, one is a member of House of Representatives, and the other three voters are electors.[8] This means that each elector represents two voters. Actual states with a small population, such as Vermont, have an elector representing about 200,000 residents (not voters). Compare this number with that of the states with larger populations, such as California or New York, where each elector represents over a half million residents. In fact, with the 2000 census and reapportionment of Congress, Wyoming, Vermont, and North Dakota will have, respectively, 165,107, 203,297, and 214,585 residents per elector. In comparison, New York, Texas, and California will have, respectively, 613,064, 614,823, and 616,924. These computations strongly suggest that rather than "one person, one vote," the Electoral College is seriously biased to give the voters from small states as much as three times more power in selecting the next President as the voters from large states.

By replacing each state's population count with the actual number of votes cast in that state in the 2000 election, a sample of the numbers of *voters* per elector follows.

| State | Voters | $\frac{\text{Voters}}{\text{Elector}}$ | State | Voters | $\frac{\text{Voters}}{\text{Elector}}$ |
|---|---|---|---|---|---|
| D.C. | 188,950 | 62,980 | Florida | 5,922,530 | 236,900 |
| Wyoming | 208,100 | 69,370 | Ohio | 4,509,800 | 214,750 |
| Alaska | 223,100 | 74,370 | Illinois | 4,636,000 | 210,730 |
| Vermont | 287,250 | 95,750 | California | 10,563,000 | 195,600 |
| N. Dakota | 280,980 | 93,660 | New York | 6,191,000 | 187,620 |

Rather than voters having equal weight in determining the leadership of the country, this table adds support to the argument that a voter from the District of Columbia, Wyoming, Alaska, or Vermont enjoyed between two

---

[7]Even if it is unlikely to eliminate the Electoral College, other reforms might be possible. Suppose, for instance, that Ralph Nader won one state; it does not matter which one. Then, as happened once before, the "House of Representatives" would select the new President rather than any procedure reflecting the voters' preferences. Such an event could happen; remember, in 1968 the third party candidate George Wallace received 46 electoral votes.

[8]The example requires six voters as an elector cannot be in the House or the Senate.

to three times more influence in the selection of the president than a voter from Florida, Ohio, Illinois, or California.

Maybe. But, then, maybe there are situations when the bias is not so radical. To examine this notion with more care, we need to measure the elusive term "political power." To develop intuition, consider a hypothetical setting (which somewhat resembles the situation for the year 2001) where the U.S. Congress is nearly tied with 217 Democrats and 218 Republicans, the U.S. Senate has 49 Democrats and 51 Republicans, and the U.S. President is a Republican. Because the Democrats and Republicans are nearly tied, a strict number counting argument suggests that the two parties have essentially equal power. This is false.

With decisions made by a majority vote and by exercising tight party discipline, this hypothetical division provides Republicans essentially dictatorial power. In reality, even though both parties would have almost the same numbers in each house, the Democrats lack the votes to affect even a single piece of legislation; they would have no influence whatsoever. This reality suggests that rather than using raw numbers to determine influence, a more accurate measure of political influence should reflect the ability to effect change. Similarly, in the Electoral College, rather than a number counting of a state's electoral votes, or the number of electors per voter, a more appropriate measure captures the state's ability to change the outcome.

To explore this issue, return to above hypothetical Congressional example and its key assumption of "tight party discipline." Such discipline can be difficult to maintain because of the strong incentives which could encourage some Republicans to defect. For purposes of illustration, suppose two Republican Congressmen and two Republican Senators leave their party to form a de facto "Consensus" Party. While this may seem silly to do, it is not. Although dwarfed in terms of numbers, the Consensus Party exercises clout far beyond that suggested by any number counting argument; they become a powerful legislative force. After all, for either the Democrats or the Republicans to pass legislation by a majority vote, they must court the pivotal Consensus support.

To move this description from the hypothetical to an actual setting, consider the relative power of the justices on the U.S. Supreme Court. Each of the nine justice does not wield one-ninth of the power; some are "more equal" than others. This is because the current court composition has Justices Rehnquist, Scalia, and Thomas forming the decidedly conservative coalition, while Justices Breyer, Ginsburg, Souter, and Stevens are viewed as being a more liberal coalition. Remaining are Justices Kennedy and O'Connor.

A court verdict requires five votes, so neither the conservative nor the more liberal coalition has the necessary votes. As Kennedy and O'Connor provide the swing votes on all divided conservative–liberal issues, they exercise a stronger say in the judiciary direction of the court. Support for these comments come from the Supreme Court deliberations about the 2000 Presidential election where press attention accurately focussed more on the views of Kennedy and O'Connor than on those of the other justices. Some pundits even argued that, rather than the American voters, these two justices selected the next President of the United States.

**1.3. Power indices.** To convert this "political power" discussion into a mathematical expression, suppose there are $N \geq 2$ players, or parties, in the "game." The gathering of players into specified coalitions assures certain gains; e.g., with five or more justices joining a coalition to express a common view, the gain achieved by the coalition is the specified court decision. More generally, let $\nu(S)$ designate the rewards accorded to coalition $S$; the meaning of "rewards" depends on what we are discussing — football victories, legislation, profits, etc.

To have more precise notation, if $\mathcal{P}$ is the list of all possible coalitions — including the empty set $\emptyset$ — of the $N$ players (that is, $\mathcal{P}$ is the power set), then $\nu$ is a mapping

$$(1) \qquad\qquad \nu : \mathcal{P} \to R$$

which describes the gains and profits, or the defeats and losses, which can be obtained by each coalition.

In the legislative example involving a majority vote, for example, where "1" means victory and "0" denotes failure,

$$(2) \qquad\qquad \nu(S) = \begin{cases} 1 & \text{if } |S| > N/2, \\ 0 & \text{if } |S| \leq N/2, \end{cases}$$

and $|S|$ is the number of players in coalition $S$. Using words, this example just means that a coalition "wins" — it has a full victory of 1 — if it has over half of the voters. So, for the Supreme Court, we have

$$\nu(S) = \begin{cases} 1 & \text{if } |S| \geq 5, \\ 0 & \text{if } |S| \leq 4. \end{cases}$$

For the Electoral College, $\nu$ becomes

$$(3) \qquad\qquad \nu(S) = \begin{cases} 1 & \text{if } |S| \geq 270, \\ 0 & \text{if } |S| \leq 269. \end{cases}$$

If the Electoral College were replaced with a direct popular vote, then

$$(4) \qquad \nu(S) = \begin{cases} 1 & \text{if } |S| \text{ is larger than any other coalition,} \\ 0 & \text{if there is a larger coalition.} \end{cases}$$

More complicated choices might have $\nu(S)$ representing the amount of money a coalition $S$ of internet entrepreneurs might earn, or the number of victories expected by a basketball team where $S$ is the roster of players.

To continue with the sports example, suppose a professional basketball team, where $S$ is a listing of the players, is expected to win 50 games this season. In our notation, this means that $\nu(S) = 50$. Suppose by adding a new player represented by $j$, say Michael Jordan, the team is expected to win 70 games. Using our notation, this means that $\nu(S \cup \{j\}) = 70$. So, the value Jordan adds to the team is the additional $\nu(S \cup \{j\}) - \nu(S) = 70 - 50 = 20$ victories.

To describe this computation more generally, whatever the gains or advantages $\nu$ represents, $\nu(S)$ describes what a coalition, a group represented by $S$, can attain on its own. If $j$ joins the group, then the new coalition is represented by $S \cup \{j\}$, and $\nu(S \cup \{j\})$ states what this enhanced group can achieve. Thus the added value of having $j$ is

$$(5) \qquad \nu(S \cup \{j\}) - \nu(S).$$

To illustrate with the Congressional example, the two players are the Democrats $D$ and Republicans $R$; they define the four coalitions

$$\mathcal{P} = \{\emptyset, \, D, \, R, \, \{D, R\}\}.$$

The majority vote $\nu$ of Eq. 2 defines the values

$$\nu(\emptyset) = \nu(D) = 0, \quad \nu(R) = \nu(\{D, R\}) = 1.$$

Using Eq. 5, computations such as

$$\nu(\{D, R\}) - \nu(R) = 1 - 1 = 0 \text{ or } \nu(D) - \nu(\emptyset) = 0 - 0 = 0$$

capture the reality that $D$'s contributions toward passage of legislation, in any imaginable situation, is zero. Their vote may enhance the final tally, but their participation is not needed. On the other hand, the computations

$$\nu(\{D, R\}) - \nu(D) = 1 - 0 = 1 \text{ and } \nu(R) - \nu(\emptyset) = 1 - 0 = 1$$

reflect the reality that the Republicans, by having over half of the votes, dominate.

Compare this setting with what happens should the the Consensus Party be formed. Here the $\nu$ values become

$$\nu(\emptyset) = \nu(C) = \nu(D) = \nu(R) = 0;$$

this just means that each party by itself cannot force the passage of any legislation. However, the values

$$\nu(\{C,D\}) = \nu(\{C,R\}) = \nu(\{D,R\}) = \nu(\{C,D,R\}) = 1$$

show that when any two parties combine, the coalition can ensure victory. To find each party's influence, similar computations using Eq. 5, such as $\nu(\{C,D\} - \nu(D) = 1$ or $\nu(\{C,D\}) - \nu(C) = 1$,[9] prove that the value any party adds by joining any other party is "1;" in particular, what empowers the Consensus Party is that, by forming a coalition, they can force a legislative victory. (The added value is zero, however, if a party joins with the other two as the victory already had been assured.)

An obvious weakness with the Eq. 5 formulation is that it fails to distinguish between who joined with whom, and it measures a player's contributions relative to only *one* coalition. Did, for instance, the Consensus Party join with the Democrats, or did the Democrats join with the Consensus Party? In the sports example, Michael Jordan provided a 20 game difference by joining a particular team. To find the overall assessment of him, we need to find the difference he would make over all possible teams — even those so good, or so bad, that his presence would not affect the victory total. To find the total power, or contributions, of a player over all possible situations, these Eq. 5 differences are averaged over all possible coalitions and all ways in which a party can join with others.

To accomplish this goal, multipliers $\lambda_S \geq 0$ are introduced to describe the relative importance, or maybe the likelihood, of certain coalitions. One choice, for instance, is to let $\lambda_S$ be a fixed reciprocal of the number of involved individuals; this choice captures the sense that a coalition which needs to satisfy more people is harder to assemble than a coalition involving smaller numbers. In the Congressional example, this would mean that

$$(6) \qquad \lambda_{C,D} = \lambda_{C,R} = \frac{1}{219}, \quad \lambda_{D,R} = \frac{1}{433}, \quad \lambda_{C,D,R} = \frac{1}{435}.$$

Widely used choices are the Shapley value (e.g., see the papers by Shapley and his coauthors [**71, 72, 73, 74**]), where $\lambda_S = 1/N\binom{N}{|S|}$ reflects the number of ways coalitions of a certain size could be established, and the Banzhaf index (Banzhaf [**5, 6**]), where $\lambda_S = 1/2^N$ uses the same weight with each coalition.

For specified $\lambda_S$ multipliers, the *power index* of player $j$ is given by

$$(7) \qquad p_j =: \sum_{S \in \mathcal{P}(j)} \lambda_{S \cup \{j\}} [\nu(S \cup \{j\}) - \nu(S)]$$

---

[9]The first computation is where the Consensus Party join the Democrats; the second is where the Democrats join with the Consensus Party.

where $\mathcal{P}(j)$ lists those coalitions which do not include player $j$. This $p_j$ value, then, describes the averaged contribution of player $j$ over all possible situations. Of course, "larger is better" as a larger $p_j$ value means that $j$ exercises more power.

To illustrate the computations with the Congressional example involving the break-away Consensus Party (where I ignore zero values such as $\nu(\{C, D, R\}) - \nu(\{D, R\})$ or $\nu(C) - \nu(\emptyset)$), we have that

$$p_C = \frac{1}{219}\{[\nu(\{C, R\}) - \nu(R)] + [\nu(\{C, D\}) - \nu(C)]\} = \frac{2}{219}$$

while

$$p_D = \frac{1}{219}[\nu(\{C, D\}) - \nu(C)] + \frac{1}{433}[\nu(\{D, R\}) - \nu(R)]\} = \frac{1}{219} + \frac{1}{433}$$

and

$$p_R = \frac{1}{219}[\nu(\{C, R\}) - \nu(C)] + \frac{1}{433}[\nu(\{D, R\}) - \nu(D)]\} = \frac{1}{219} + \frac{1}{433}.$$

These numbers suggest that although small in numbers, the pivotal Consensus Party is about four-thirds as strong as either "major" party!

Does it make sense for a small group of Republicans to retain their party affiliation, but to break away from "Republican party policy" on various issues to form a de facto "Consensus Swing Party?" It sure does, at least in the short run. By doing so, they gain considerable power in influencing legislation. While our legislators may not recognize the formal presentation, they fully appreciate the intuitive aspects of this argument. For this reason, on varying issues of concern, expect to witness informal tactics resembling a "Consensus Party" which would temper the wishes of the dominant party. Even though the Republicans of our hypothetical example could, theoretically, exercise dictatorial rule, such complete dominance cannot be expected with reasonably balanced parties.[10]

A similar analysis with the Supreme Court example where the players are the Conservatives, Liberals, and Justices Kennedy and O'Connor demonstrates the added power of the last two swing voters — at least in situations where the conservative and liberal blocks are at odds. This is dramatically demonstrated in certain issues of women rights where Justice O'Connor can break a usual 4-4 tie in ways she sees fit.

**1.4. Back to the Electoral College.** Measuring power, or influence, in selecting the next President in the Electoral College, then, is more complicated than just a number counting argument citing the number of residents

---

[10]A more realistic legislative model, which explains why legislation in a nearly balanced Senate is more moderate, must include the power of a party to filibuster. If the dominant party does not have the votes to close discussion, they must compromise with the minor party to pass new laws.

per elector. A more accurate measure would involve computing all circumstances when a state's electors make the decisive difference in the outcome. The key element is the "all circumstances" phrase. Rather than limiting attention to the actual order in which each state's votes are tallied, all possible ways of lining up the states to count their ballots must be considered.

When determining the power of the state of South Dakota, for instance, there are many ways to sum the electoral votes by starting with South Dakota. Then, there are many other orderings where South Dakota's votes are counted second, or third, or .... So, to find the power of South Dakota, out of all possible arrangements of adding the different state's electoral votes, we want to compute the number of arrangements where South Dakota's votes make the deciding difference at the precise point when they are included. Clearly, if the ordering adds South Dakota's three votes near the beginning of the process, the votes contribute to the conclusion but do not decide the outcome. There are, however, a limited number of arrangements where South Dakota's votes happened to be added at the critical juncture; these are the settings where South Dakota's vote decides the next President. The state's actual power can be viewed as the number of times this happens.

Difficult computations are not needed. Only in those limited number of arrangements where the state's votes are added to a partial tally of 267, or 268, or 269 does South Dakota make the decisive difference. Compare this with what would happen for, say, the state of Florida with its 25 electoral votes; Florida would make the decisive difference for any counting arrangement where, when its electoral votes are added, the partial tally is anywhere between 245 and 269. (In 2000, the partial tally was 246.) Clearly, settings favoring Florida occur far more often than those favoring South Dakota.

1.4.1. *From a nail-biter to a close call.* This counting shows that when measuring a state's power, the answer depends upon the particular situation. In the nail-biting 2000 election, Bush won with 271 electoral votes. Had any state with a close outcome favoring Bush, such as Arkansas, New Hampshire, Tennessee, or West Virginia, voted in a different manner, the outcome would have switched. Consequently, in this election, each state supporting Bush enjoyed equal power. But if *each state* had equal influence in determining the conclusion, then each voter from a small population state which supported Bush, such as Wyoming, enjoyed nearly three times more influence in determining the election conclusion than voters from Florida or Texas. Although all attention focussed on Florida, the Bush camp should be thanking the ignored but surprisingly powerful Wyoming voter.

This nail-biting election resembles a razor-thin basketball victory — when credit is distributed, even that small sub in his first game making only three points at a crucial moment must accorded the same credit as the huge star with around 30 points. Pursuing this sports analogy, there are two other natural Electoral College settings. The first one mimics a close, but not nail-biting sports victory; while the star's role is more noticeable, the sub's contribution remains valuable. Similarly, when the Electoral College winner receives about 300 to 310 votes, the role played by the large state is enhanced, but support from the small states remains useful.

To avoid becoming mired in messy number-crunching, consider the simple case where Smith's Electoral College votes come from state $C$'s (intended to suggest California) five votes and from the nine other states of $V$ (intended to suggest Vermont), $E$, $F$, $G$, $H$, $I$, $J$, $K$, and $L$ which have one vote each. If each small state has 10,000 residents while $C$ has a 100,000 population, then each small state has 10,000 residents per electoral vote while $C$ appears to be underrepresented with $100,000/5 = 20,000$ residents per electoral vote. These numbers suggest that $C$ voters have only half the influence as those from other states.

Now, compare the influence levels in terms of power. Suppose Smith needs nine votes to win. The only way a small state, $V$, can make the deciding decision is by joining a coalition with precisely eight votes. Thus, $V$ makes the difference only when joining the coalition of all small states, or a coalition with $C$ and three small states; it could be "$C, E, F, G$," or "$C, E, F, H$," or .... There are 57 different arrangements; all other coalitions either have insufficient votes, or the decision already is made.

State $C$, on the other hand, experiences a larger range of possibilities; it just needs to join a coalition having anywhere between four to eight votes. So, $C$ ensures victory in 381 different ways. Thus, when measuring influence and power, although $C$ has five times more votes than $V$, $C$ actually is about $381/57 = 6.684$ times more powerful in the selection of the President. Thus, $C$ enjoys having $100,000/6.684 = 14,961$ residents per power unit, while $V$ and the other states have 10,000 residents per power unit. Here, the situation comes closer to parity. The decrease in $V$'s influence reflects the fact that its vote is useful, but not as crucial as in a nail-biting election.

Turning to the actual Electoral College, suppose both Vermont and California support the winner who receives somewhere about 300 or 310 electoral votes. Vermont's influence is determined by those rare arrangements where Vermont's three electoral votes are counted just when the partial tally is 267, 268, or 269. Even more limiting than our example, each of these coalitions must include California. California, however, makes the deciding difference for the wider range where the partial tally is anywhere between 216 and 269. Again, as in the example, in many of these arrangements Vermont's vote can be replaced with that from some other state. Consequently, all of these added ways in which California makes the difference adds to the state's influence in selecting the President. This, in turn, increases a Californian voter's influence in selecting the President.

1.4.2. *A blow-out.* The last Electoral College victory, of the magnitude enjoyed by Ronald Reagan, is motivated by a sports' blow-out. In reading the morning paper describing how one team wiped out another, the star will receive more press than that forgotten sub. To see what can happen in influence levels, modify the above example by having three more states, each with one vote, also support Smith.

Again, for $V$ to make the difference, it must join a coalition with precisely eight votes. It could be with $C$ and three other states, or with eight of the other eleven small states; there are 330 ways for this to happen. State $C$, on the other hand, can join any coalition which has between six and ten votes; there are 3498 choices. This setting *enhances* $C$'s power to $3498/330 = 10.6$ times that of the smaller states. Consequently, there are about $100,000/10.6 = 9434$ residents per power unit, so the $C$ voter now has slightly more influence than a voter from the other states.

Returning to the Electoral College and by using arguments involving areas under different portions of that ever-so-familiar "bell-shaped curve," it turns out that California exercises more than $54/3 = 18$ more power than Vermont in selecting a President, but not that much more. In other words, *a voter in a small state has two to three times more influence in selecting an* elector *than a voter from a large state. However, as we move away from a nail-biting, razor-close election, the influence of a voter in selecting the* President *increases.*[11] While the real power of a voter from California *for electing the President, not an elector,* appears to remain less than that of a voter from Vermont, the Californian voter enjoys more influence than suggested by the simplistic number counting argument.

1.4.3. *Real power.* So, the power of a larger state is greater than what we normally expect. This is not an academic exercise; the 2000 election is the first time since 1976 that California has not voted for the new President. Now extend this argument to political hardball where legislation, Presidential appointments, and other goodies are partially designed to attract voters for the next Presidential election. While some of the smaller states who supported Gore, such as Hawaii and Delaware, and maybe even Massachusetts, might realistically worry about some "benign neglect" during a Bush administration, the electoral-rich California does not share the same level of concern. California's rich power coming from its 55 electoral votes (after the 2000 census) makes it a highly attractive prize for both parties. This

---

[11]This phrase and material in this section are based on conversations with Katri Sieberg.

reality was manifested even before the Bush inauguration where the important cabinet post of secretary of agriculture, which usually goes to someone from the midwest, was given to Ann Veneman — from California.

Veneman was later joined by the appointments of two other Californians, Norman Mineta, as secretary of transportation and Anthony Principi for veteran affairs, but there are just two Texans on the cabinet. Moreover, watch what happens should California suffer a serious setback; most surely there will be attempts to use it to embarrass the state's Democratic governor, but also expect actions to curry favor with voters. The electoral vote status of California is captured by that old joke about where a 600 pound gorilla can sit "anywhere it wants!"

**1.5. Popular vote and other reforms.** Now return to the widely endorsed proposal of having a *popular vote election*. Without the protection of the Electoral College, a similar argument shows that the influence of a small state becomes miniscule. After all, the 404,000 Californian votes cast for Ralph Nader, the Green Party candidate, exceeded the number of all voters in each of several of the smaller states. Without the protection of the Electoral College, voters from sparsely populated regions would be, essentially, ignored.

Of course, the elimination of the Electoral College is only one possible reform. But many of the other "reform approaches" will encounter resistance for similar political power reasons. A potential solution for this Presidential election difficulty, for instance, is to follow the lead of the states of Maine and Nebraska[12] by having the electors from each state roughly apportioned to the different candidates according to the number of popular votes they receive. In the year 2000 Florida elections, this would mean that the 25 electoral votes would have been split almost equally between Bush and Gore.

Such a procedure would make it more unlikely for the winners of the popular vote and the Electoral College to differ. Moreover, such a change would not face the daunting challenge of requiring a Constitutional amendment; this procedural decision is left to the discretion of individual states. Yet while the proposal makes sense, in the absence of strong public and political pressure and incentives, I would be shocked if such a reform would be adopted by many states. This is because the same "power argument" shows that this division would diminish a state's power in determining the election outcome. A state offering only 10, rather than its full 18 electoral votes, loses decisive power in determining the election. For electoral reform, we need to look elsewhere.

---

[12]In these states, one elector goes to the winner of each congressional district. The last two electors (which represent the two senators) go to the winner of the state.

## 2. Other procedures

Even before November, 2000, it was widely accepted that the election between Bush and Gore would be close, very close. Beyond the usual "get-out-the-vote" tactics of the major parties, even the media warned about the importance of voting and the difference it would make.

One humorous but striking media message appeared in the popular cartoon strip *Doonesbury* on election day. Each of the first panels displayed different characters listening to a radio announcer repeating some of the charges and fears Gore and Nader supporters aimed at the Bush candidacy.

- "If you'd like to see abortion re-criminalized ... "
- "If you're for unrestrained logging and drilling, and for voluntary pollution control ... "
- "and if you favor more soft money in politics, then the choice today is clear ... "
- "Vote Nader."

The point of the warning was that if many of the voters who preferred Gore to Bush voted for their first choice of Nader, then Bush would win. What an accurate prophecy; this is precisely what happened.

The real problem with the 2000 election was not chads or questionable absentee ballots; it was the candidacy of Ralph Nader. Bush beat Gore in New Hampshire by less than 8,000 votes, but Nader received about 22,000 New Hampshire votes. In the controversial, hotly contested state of Florida where Bush bested Gore by only hundreds of votes, Nader received about 97,000 votes. Had the Nader voters voted for one of the two major candidates, and if this vote had split as exit polls and many others predicted, Gore would have comfortably won both states — and he would have won the Presidency.

But it is wrong to blame Nader or his supporters for the election outcome. In a democracy, anyone can run for office; anyone can vote for whom they wish. Nader's goal was not to win the Presidency; beyond using the election as a means to promote his message, a main objective was his unsuccessful attempt to achieve 5% of the total vote so that the Green Party would qualify for federal funding during the next Presidential election. In fact, as a twist on the traditional argument, perhaps the Green Party members should blame Gore for the failure of their party to reach the 5% barrier. This is because, rather than voting for Nader, many Nader supporters strategically voted for their second choice of Gore.

**2.1. A better approach?** The problem is not dangling chads, or absentee ballots, or the Supreme Court, or Bush, or Gore, or Nader; it is our flawed election procedure. With even a slightly improved election approach, all of this mess could have been avoided. To demonstrate by considering just one alternative approach, suppose each state used an "Instant Runoff Procedure."

This method is not new; under the name of the "Second Choice" procedure, it was used in the Wisconsin state primaries[13] way back in 1912 and 1914. The procedure closely resembles a traditional runoff except that, instead of holding a second runoff election at another date, voters provide the information needed to instantly hold a runoff. As used in the recent mayoral elections of London, England, each voter lists on the ballot his or her top- and second-choice candidates. But the ballot need not be limited to two choices; three, or four, or as many as desired could be rank ordered. This is what happens in the election for the President of Ireland, the approach currently being experimented with in the Berkeley City Council, and this method was even suggested as the fair way to select a "survivor" in a so-called "real-life" TV series.

The election is first tallied by using only the voters' first-place votes. If no candidate receives a majority, then all but the top two candidates are eliminated, and the ballots are recounted. In the recount, or runoff, if a voter's first-place candidate remains in contention, that is the tallied vote. If a voter's preferred candidate is eliminated, then the voter's second choice is counted. As applied to a presidential election, the winner of this procedure would receive the state's electoral votes.

It is easy to understand why such a procedure could be warmly embraced across the spectrum starting from the supporters of Ralph Nader to those of Pat Buchanan (a minor "Reform Party" candidate in the 2000 presidential election who is on the conservative side of the political spectrum). The advantage for a Nader supporter, for instance, is that this method might have permitted Nader to receive the desired 5% of the vote. This is because, without fear of the "Doonesbury penalty," a Nader voter could sincerely place Nader in first place, and then list her or his preferred major candidate in the second position. The tallies from the first election would indicate the level of Nader's support; the outcome of the runoff would determine the winner of the electoral votes. Moreover, the runoff provision would have removed doubt whether the election outcome reflected the voters' wishes, or the woeful limitations of the election procedure. In the 2000 election, the

---

[13]My thanks to Steve Barney, from Oshkosh, Wisconsin, for calling this historical fact, and the reference of "Wisconsin Statutes, 1913, Chapter 5, Section 11–12.8, p. 27," to my attention. As Barney writes, "It was put in place by the progressives, and repealed by the conservatives. ... [In one election with several progressive candidates, most] voters neglected to indicate any second choice candidate. As a consequence, a conservative gubernatorial candidate, Phillips, beat a bunch of progressives in the 1914 Republican primary, and that conservative governor then led the push to repeal [the procedure]."

runoff would have been invoked for the eight states of Florida, Iowa, Maine, Minnesota, New Hampshire, New Mexico, Oregon, and Wisconsin.

Is this the "best" procedure? Does it suffer flaws or weaknesses?[14] It sure does: many of them. In a later chapter, for instance, I show that it is possible to have more voters showing up to support the winning candidate, and the candidate now loses! These kinds of questions will be discussed. But first, we need a partial listing of possible election methods.

**2.2. Voting methods and class standings.** A serious stumbling block in understanding elections and election procedures is the dramatic conceptual gap between allowing the voters to more accurately express their opinions, and ensuring that the societal election outcome accurately reflects the voters' wishes. Are these goals compatible, or is there a potential conflict?

This issue is often raised. Long ago, for instance, I learned to anticipate that, after I lecture about voting procedures, someone in the audience will propose the "novel" procedure of giving each voter a fixed number of points, say 10. The voter can then distribute these points among the candidates in a manner which, presumably, reflects the voter's preferences. How can anyone argue against an election approach which allows a voter to more accurately distinguish his or her personal views about the alternatives?

Notice how this "division of points" method places all emphasis on the opinions and wishes of individual voters. Replacing any discussion about how this could affect the election outcome is the tacit assumption that optimizing the freedom of expression of the voters also optimizes the accuracy of the societal election outcome. But is this true? Paradoxically, could allowing voters to more accurately reflect their individual beliefs result in a societal outcome which inaccurately represents all voters' true beliefs? Surprisingly, this is the case.

In the later chapters, approaches will be developed which show the consequences of using certain procedures. But a more intuitive introduction is useful. Therefore, to create a distinction between the voter's options and the integrity of the society outcome, let me use an analogy that all of us can understand and appreciate — it involves ways to determine the class standing of students.

---

[14]An immediate one has a minor candidate encouraging enough voters to strategically list him or her first just "to send a message" — and then winning the election to the voters' dismay. This is not a hypothetical warning. In the 1972 Illinois gubernatorial election, many Democrats wanted to "send a message" to Chicago Mayor Richard Daley by voting for someone other than his choice, even though his candidate was accepted as being reasonable. The goal was for Daley's candidate to win, but by a smaller vote. So many voters adopted this strategy, however, that the other candidate, Dan Walker, won both the primary and general election. Later Walker was indicted for financial wrong doing.

In what follows, different hypothetical "class ranking" approaches are introduced. When posed in terms of academic procedures, weaknesses can become apparent. After the strengths and weaknesses of a ranking method are briefly described, the associated voting procedure is defined. In this comparison, "students" represent "candidates," and the "instructor of each course" represents a "voter." To be sure that the terminology is familiar, recall that the standard grading procedure uses

- an "A" to represent excellence,
- a "B" to denote good work,
- a "C" to capture the sense of average work,
- a "D" to mean poor work, and
- an "F" to designate failure.

2.2.1. *Class standing via excellence.* Since a student's class standing should represent her or his level of excellence, it seems reasonable to place all emphasis on the number of A's a student earns. Following this philosophy, suppose that tomorrow morning the principal of a local school announces that, from now on, class standings will be based solely on the number of A's a student receives.

How unjust! While a superficial examination suggests that this method rewards excellence, in reality, this warped procedure promotes obvious inequities. It ranks, for instance, a student with 5 A's and 39 F's above a student with 4 A's and 40 B's. In other words, this method allows a weaker student to be higher ranked. The obvious source of weakness of this ranking procedure is that, by only concentrating on A's, it ignores the wealth of available information about a student's performance in each course.

*Plurality vote.* The election ranking procedure corresponding to this ranking approach is the standard *plurality* method used across the world. This is where each voter votes for one candidate. The candidate receiving the largest number of votes wins. As with the academic ranking method, information about whom a voter has second, third, ... , and last ranked is ignored.

But which plurality elections are suspect? The class ranking scenario, where a student with many F's is ranked above one with many B's, suggests that we should worry about any plurality election where a candidate who is top ranked by a solid core of supporters also is bottom ranked by many others. Maybe because of the tension which can accompany an election, or the need for a candidate to be distinguished from the others, this division of the vote is surprisingly common. In the 1996 Republican Presidential primaries in New Hampshire, the underdog candidate Pat Buchanan enjoyed the core support of nearly 30% of the voters. However, the polls and press commentaries indicated that Buchanan had a "love him, or hate him" controversial image where well over half of the voters had Buchanan ranked at, or near, the bottom. Using the grading analogy, Buchanan had a reasonable number of A's with a sizeable number of F's. On the other hand, Robert Dole, the favorite and eventual Presidential candidate for the Republican party, was highly regarded by most voters. With the grading analogy, Dole's reasonable number of A's was supported by many B's. To the surprise of many, and the consternation of the Republican party hoping for party unity leading into the 1996 Presidential campaign, Buchanan won the primary. The reason for his election is clear; the voting procedure counted only the A's and ignored all other information about how voters compared Buchanan and Dole.

A similar situation occurred in the 1998 gubernatorial election in Minnesota. As a popular radio show reminds us, this is a state where one can expect to find Norwegian bachelor farmers walking along dusty roads; it is a state where the women are strong and all the children are above average. This is a state which belongs to that portion of the midwest known for preferring seasoned leadership, rather than novices, to run the state government. For these reasons, candidate Hubert "Skip" Humphrey III, an effective state's attorney general, was the strong favorite to win the election. The Republican candidate, the seasoned and highly respected Norm Coleman, was expected to do reasonably well. Both candidates took lightly the Reform Party candidate Jesse Ventura. After all, even by Ventura's own admission, he was not that clear about all of the functioning of the state government and his experience had been limited to being mayor of a small suburb, a professional wrestler, and a talk-radio host.

While Ventura's considerable charisma and "straight-talk" allowed him to be top ranked by about 37% of the voters, there is reason to suspect that well over half of the voters preferred both Humphrey and Coleman to Ventura. In other words, while Ventura had more A's than either Humphrey or Coleman, he also had a sizeable number of C's. In comparison, both Humphrey and Coleman received a sizeable number of A's and B's. In fact, it is reasonable to expect that Ventura would have lost to either of the other candidates in a head-to-head election. But since this extra ranking information about the voters' preferences is totally ignored by our standard voting procedure, Ventura won the plurality election.

For a less extreme example, recall that a scenario coming from the "class ranking" ranks a student with 10 A's and some B's and C's above a student with 9 A's and many more B's. This example accurately suggests that the plurality election approach can cause the defeat of a candidate who is first and second ranked by many voters; the candidate can lose because the "second-ranked" votes don't count. One example is Dole's failure to win the

1996 New Hampshire Republican primary. A dramatic recent illustration is the 2000 Presidential election where Nader's candidacy prompted many voters to place Gore in second place; this caused Gore to lose the election.

A third example, which illustrates how voting procedures extend beyond politics into sports, comes from the 1994 Winter Olympic Games in Lille-hammer, Norway. While most memories of this event are forever tied to the earlier assault on the skater Nancy Kerrigan by associates of rival Tonya Harding, these clubbing events need not detain us as we move straight to the final event where the sixteen-year-old Ukrainian orphan Oksana Baiul beat Kerrigan for the gold medal. But did she? Or was this another manifestation of an inadequate voting procedure?

While the ranking procedure for figure skating is sophisticated, it is not necessarily reliable. The problems do not arise from all of those confusing 5.8s and 5.9s which we actively scan and compare after each skater leaves the ice — think of them as worksheet numbers that are used to determine each judge's final ranking of all skaters. Rather, the problem is caused by how the judges' rankings are combined. Just as with the grading story, the final outcome need not be their true cumulative intent.

While I confess that Oksana Baiul was my favorite in the Lillehammer Olympics, I also believe that the judges' scores, which are listed in the following table, indicate that Nancy Kerrigan, who placed second behind Baiul, was their true collective favorite. What complicates the issue are the scores for the third skater Chen Lu, who won China's first medal, a bronze, in figure skating. By skating so well, Chen Lu tossed some "C grades" into the scoring mix.

|          | Ger. | Pol. | Czech. | Ukr. | China | U.S. | Jap. | Can. | U.K. |
|----------|------|------|--------|------|-------|------|------|------|------|
| Baiul    | 1    | 1    | 1      | 1    | 1     | 2    | 2    | 3    | 3    |
| Kerrigan | 2    | 2    | 2      | 2    | 2     | 1    | 1    | 1    | 1    |
| Chen Lu  | 3    | 3    | 3      | 3    | 3     | 3    | 3    | 2    | 2    |

These rankings are based on rules governing how much weight is assigned to a judge's evaluation of technical skills vs. artistic impression; indeed, with these rules, at least one of Baiul's first-place rankings was a very close call.

Once the rankings are determined, the winner is based on a plurality vote among those candidates who are ranked number one. In this Olympics, the method awarded first place to Oksana Baiul by a narrow 5–4 vote. But using the class ranking story, we have to wonder. After all Baiul received only one more "A" than Kerrigan, but she received two C's whereas Kerrigan's lowest grades are B's. A bit more about this Olympic ranking is stated later.

2.2.2. *Punishing failure.* At the far extreme from a "count only the A's" is where the goal is to penalize failures. Here, a class standing is determined strictly by counting the number of F's a student receives where more F's means a poorer ranking. An equivalent approach, which could be dismissed as a political spin to make the approach more socially acceptable, is to count the number of grades a student has above an F, and then rank the students accordingly. It is not necessary to create any stories suggesting the limitations of this approach; its weaknesses are obvious. It ranks, for instance, a student with straight D's above that student who earned straight A's in all courses except for that one F in gym.

*Antiplurality vote.* The corresponding election procedure is called the *antiplurality vote.* One version of this procedure asks each voter to vote *against* one candidate (hence, the "antiplurality" name); to tally the ballots, that candidate is given "$-1$" points. An alternative, equivalent approach is to have the voter vote for all but one candidate. In either case, the candidates are ranked according to the number of points received. By reviewing the grading story, it is clear how this procedure can elect a candidate that the voters view as being beneath mediocrity. Yet we often use this method; on a personnel committee, for instance, how often do we start by "eliminating" candidates.

2.2.3. *Count A's and B's and ... .* Closely related ranking schemes are to select a cut-off grade, and then count all grades a student earns above the threshold. For instance, maybe the class standing is determined by the number of A's and B's a student has; all C's, D's and F's are to be ignored. Remember, no distinction is to be made between whether a grade is an A or a B. Or, maybe the cutoff is between a C and D; here a count is made of the number of A's, B's, C's a student has (no distinction is made among these grades) and this number is used to determine the class standing. The earlier methods where only A's are counted, or where only F's are not counted, are special cases. Again, because valued information is being ignored and because distinctions are not being made about different levels of performance, it is easy to create all sorts of examples indicating serious weaknesses of these approaches.

*Vote for k-candidates.* Variants of the corresponding election methods are widely used. How often have we had a ballot asking us to vote for two, or for three candidates? These approaches suffer all of the problems suggested by what can go wrong with the associated grading method.

2.2.4. *Teacher's choice.* A radical approach to determine class rankings combines all of the above. But here, the precise choice about who is listed for academic honors is strictly based on each teacher's opinion about each student. Here is the rub; there is no uniform standard. As such, some teachers might list the student only if she or he earned an A in the course. Another teacher might choose to include a student who barely received a C, while a third teacher might state that a D suffices. This approach even allows a teacher to list a student's name no matter what grade is earned — even an F. Remember, only a list of names is supplied; no distinction is made about any students' grades. In fact, even with a C cutoff, the teacher may decide to list a student with an F for "encouragement."

Wow! This procedure adopts the weaknesses of all of the above approaches (when all teachers use the same standard) plus introducing randomness into the outcome (when different teachers at different times use different standards)! As a result of all of this flexibility offered the teachers, we should strongly suspect that with the same students' grades almost any class standing could emerge; it would just depend upon what each teacher decides to do. By this I mean that a student top ranked with one selection could be bottom ranked with another selection. In fact, it is not clear what such a class standing means.

*Approval Voting.* The corresponding election procedure was invented by Robert Weber in 1971 as part of his Yale University Ph. D. thesis; Weber called it *Approval Voting.* While Weber subsequently wrote a couple of papers about this method, much of the analysis and promotion of Approval Voting, which includes a book by the same name [13], is due to the well-regarded research team of Steven Brams, a political scientist at New York University, and Peter Fishburn, a member of the Bell Laboratory research unit. This method allows each voter to vote "approval" for as many candidates as desired — no distinction is made about how the voter ranks the candidates.

The grading story tells us that there are ways for each student to be highly, or poorly, ranked depending on what the teachers decide to do, so we must expect that with the same voter preferences an Approval Voting election outcome can swing, radically, depending on how the voters vote approval. Later (starting on page 53), geometric tools are introduced which make it easy to prove that even if an election is not closely contested, it is uncomfortably easy and possible for any of the candidates to be elected. In fact, appropriate scenarios can be described where Ross Perot could have won the 1992 U.S. Presidential election, or (while highly unlikely) Ralph Nader could have been elected in 2000.

Currently, this method is used primarily by professional societies. This list includes the American Mathematical Society (AMS) , the Mathematical Association of America (MAA), and the Society for Social Choice & Welfare (SC&W). However, after this method was adopted by the MAA but before their first election, the president of the MAA realized the dangers associated with this method. Perhaps fearful about the possible distortions in election outcomes, he took the highly unusual step of including a warning both on the ballot and in an article (Gillman [**20**]) about how to vote with this approach. "[S]uppose there are three candidates of whom two are outstanding. Suppose the third is a person you believe is not yet ready for office but whom you decide to vote for as a means of encouragement (in addition to voting for your favorite). If enough voters reason that way, you will elect that person now."

Other scenarios associated with "teacher choice" class rankings identify associated election settings where Approval Voting outcomes are questionable. Indeed, about the only setting where at least the top-ranked student is a reasonable "teacher choice" selection arises when a particular student receives straight A's; the rest of the class ranking remains questionable. This class ranking analogy suggests that one should worry about the Approval Voting outcomes for any setting other than where there is essentially unanimous acceptance.

There are, of course, settings with nearly unanimous election outcomes. For instance, nobody is overly surprised about announcements of a nearly unanimous vote coming from dictatorial societies. Less threatening examples include professional organizations where it is rare to encounter a highly contested election. Indeed, often the vote in a professional society merely serves to validate a proposed slate. The point is that in such near unanimity settings, the choice of a procedure probably does not matter. Later (starting on page 53), however, there is a description of the contested 1999 Social Choice & Welfare election outcome where it is debatable whether the Approval Voting outcome accurately reflects the voters' wishes.

*Cumulative voting.* A procedure related both to Approval Voting and to the "division of points" method is called *cumulative voting.* This procedure, made popular with the 1993 controversy about Lani Guinier's appointment to the Justice Department, is where a voter is given a specified number of points, say two. The voter could "bullet vote" by casting both points for one candidate, or the voter could elect to cast one vote for each of two different candidates. Scenarios where this procedure could lead to questionable outcomes follow from the grading analogy where a teacher can twice list a student who received an A, or decide to list students with A's and B's.

2.2.5. *The four-point grading system.* With five grades, a traditional approach is to assign points to grades; four points for each A, three for each B, two for each C, one for each D, and zero for each F. Students are ranked according to the average number of points they receive.

We might wonder what is special about using this particular scheme. Why not assign six points for each A, four for each B, three for each C, one for each D, and zero for each F. What about other scoring weights?

*The Borda Count (BC).* The academic study of voting procedures was started in 1770 by the French mathematician Jean Charles de Borda. Borda, who had a varied research agenda with an emphasis on areas such as mathematical astronomy and fluid dynamics, criticized the election procedure used at that time — the plurality vote — to select members for the French Academy of Sciences. He proposed a weighted voting system where, for three candidates, a voter's top-, second-, and bottom-ranked candidates are assigned, respectively, 2, 1, 0 points. More generally, for $n$ candidates, the *Borda Count* (BC) assigns $n - j$ points to a voter's $j$th-ranked candidate. For several years this method was used by the French Academy. But then a new member with considerable political clout — Napoleon Bonaparte — had it changed. The analogy with the four-point class ranking approach does not suggest faults or strengths of this election method, so comments are deferred until after the material in subsequent chapters is developed.

Incidentally, Deanna Haunsperger, a mathematician at Carleton College, proved that the Kruskal-Wallis test in non-parametric statistics is closely related to the BC [**22**]. Some of her work is described in Chapter 6.

Continuing into sports, if the Borda procedure had been used in the Lillehammer Olympics, Kerrigan would have won. Using a "reversed" Borda Count where one point is given to a first-place ranking, two for a second, and so forth, and where a smaller score is better, Kerrigan, Baiul, and Chen Lu would have received, respectively, 14, 15, and 25 points to crown Kerrigan, rather than Baiul, with the gold medal.

*Positional methods.* After Borda introduced his voting method, other members of the Academy, such as the mathematician Laplace, wondered what was so special about that particular choice. Instead of 2, 1, 0, why not use 6, 5, 0, or any other choice from the continuum of possibilities? These questions led to what now is known as *positional methods:* a class of procedures which includes the BC, plurality vote, antiplurality vote, and so forth as special cases.

In this approach a specified number of points are assigned to candidates according to how they are *positioned* on a voter's ballot. If these points are $w_1 \geq w_2 \geq \cdots \geq w_n$ where $w_1 > w_n$, then $w_j$ points are assigned to a voter's $j$th-ranked candidate. For the plurality vote, $w_1 = 1$ and $w_j = 0$ for all $j > 1$. For the BC, $w_j = n - j$. While the above analogies already suggest why $w_j$ choices restricted to one and zero are flawed, it is not clear how to compare the other choices. In fact, this has formed a major research puzzle since the late eighteenth century.

The complexity of this issue created the resigned attitude shared by the field which was aptly captured by "[t]he choice of a positional voting method is subjective" attitude expressed by William Riker [**38**], a highly regarded researcher in this field. Recently another leader in this field argued that "[g]iven all the logical barriers that have to be scaled to even come close to making a coherent [argument supporting who should be the winner in an election], demanding a full ordering is a tall order." Indeed, trying to find a full ordering is "something that most of us long ago gave up on as impossible and/or incoherent." While his thoughts probably reflect the general sense of the choice community, these concerns now have answers which are described in the later chapters.

*2.2.6. Pairwise comparisons.* Although labor intensive, why not rank students according to how each student ranks relative to each other student. With Heili and Ingrid, for instance, count the number of courses where Heili does better than Ingrid, and the number where Ingrid does better than Heili; this number determines who does better than whom.

*Condorcet method.* In the mid-1780s, the French mathematician, philosopher, and politician Marie-Jean-Antoine-Nicolas de Caritat Condorcet disagreed with Borda's approach. He proposed comparing candidates in pairwise majority votes. In honor of Condorcet's contributions, a candidate who beats all other candidates is called the *Condorcet winner;* a candidate who loses to all other candidates is called the *Condorcet loser.* The Condorcet method has such appeal that it has been widely adopted as the standard for this research area. On the other hand, because the approach is overly labor intensive to compute outcomes, it is not used very often. But it still stands as the standard used to compare other approaches.

What can go wrong with the Condorcet approach? Actually, quite a bit. But they are sufficiently subtle that it takes the symmetry arguments developed in Chapter 5 to detect what they are.

**2.3. Arrow's result.** The list of procedures can go on and on. Procedures can be invented which use portions of the above at different steps. A runoff election, for instance, is where a pairwise election is used with the two candidates who are top ranked in a plurality election. The "instant" version is where voters provide enough information so all of this can be done with one ballot. The "split ten points" method is a variant of the positional methods where each voter is permitted to select the particular $w_j$ weights used to tally his or her ballot.

The fascinating rules of ice skating reflect the various attempts to correct all sorts of abuse from previous years, abuse based on strategic voting where a judge "helps" a favored skater. As already indicated, all those numbers that are flashed on the screen after a figure skating performance should be viewed as scores on a quiz or test; they are not used directly to determine the winner. Instead, these "cardinals" determine each judge's ranking of the skaters; these individual rankings are used, with a variant of the plurality vote, to determine the group's ranking of the skaters. For instance, only those skaters ranked number one by some judge is eligible to be the "winner." A skater with a majority of top ranks wins. If nobody qualifies, then second rankings of the skaters now are treated as top rankings and the process is used to find a majority vote winner.

By using the analogy of class rankings, the reader probably can conjecture all sorts of situations which would cause various procedures to have a questionable election outcome. The point is that once we start examining the issues, we begin to recognize that our standard procedures can suffer all sorts of difficulties.

But, if so many things can go wrong with standard procedures, then why not try to discover new approaches which are immune to these problems. To do so, why not create an "election procedure sieve." In other words, why not start by specifying the particular properties we want an election method to satisfy, and then identify all procedures which satisfy these conditions. Such a project was initiated by Kenneth Arrow [2].

It is useful to describe Arrow's conclusions if only because so many people (including economists, mathematicians, and political scientists) invoked this theorem to explain away the 2000 election outcome. While partially correct, all of the comments that I read had conceptual errors. So, to conclude this chapter, this important theorem is briefly described from the perspective of mathematics. Then, in Chapter 5, some of the common misconceptions are corrected. (A more complete, relatively nontechnical description of Arrow's result and "what it really means" is the focus of my book [60] "Decisions and Elections; Explaining the Unexpected.")

To describe Arrow's result, which played a role in his 1972 Nobel Prize in Economics, treat the sought-after election procedures as mappings. This means the domain (space of voter preferences), range (space of societal outcomes), and basic properties of the mappings (the election procedures) need to be described.

2.3.1. *Arrow's Theorem.*        **Domain — voter preferences**

There are only two assumptions about a voter's preferences.

1. Each voter's binary rankings of the candidates form a complete, strict, transitive ranking. This means that for any two candidates, say Jane and Kathleen, a voter prefers one over the other. Then, for any three candidates, say Jane, Kathleen, and Lorraine, if a voter prefers

Jane to Kathleen (denoted as "Jane $\succ$ Kathleen") and Kathleen $\succ$ Lorraine, then the voter also prefers Jane $\succ$ Lorraine.

2. There are no restrictions on how the voter can rank the candidates.

Before moving on to Arrow's other conditions, this is an appropriate place to introduce some terminology.

**Definition 1.** A *profile* **p** is a listing of each voter's ranking of the candidates.

To illustrate the definition, suppose, for instance, that a five-member personnel committee has to rank the applicants Mary, Nancy, and Sue for the one tenure-track position. The associated five-voter profile **p** might be where committee members Clark, Elton, and Jeff rank the candidates as "Mary $\succ$ Sue $\succ$ Nancy" while George and Mark share the "Nancy $\succ$ Mary $\succ$ Sue" ranking. This profile is later used to illustrate a property of procedures.

### Range — societal rankings

There is only one assumption about the societal rankings.

1. The societal ranking is transitive. This ranking, however, need not be strict; ties are permitted.

### Mapping — election procedure

The two basic assumptions about the election procedure are designed to prevent obvious election paradoxes.

1. **Pareto.** The first condition is named after the Italian engineer Vilfredo Pareto who introduced several mathematical tools into the analysis of economics. This condition is an unanimity requirement. Namely, if all voters share the same ranking of a pair of candidates, then the common ranking should be the election outcome. To illustrate with our five-voter example, as everyone prefers Mary to Sue, that should be their relative societal ranking. This is the *Pareto* condition.

2. **Independence from Irrelevant Alternatives** (IIA). Suppose a committee charged with ranking three candidate for the one tenure-track position decides on the ranking Monica $\succ$ Naomi $\succ$ Olinda. When questioned at a departmental meeting, the committee chair confessed that if fewer committee members had liked Olinda, then they would have ranked Naomi above Monica. Doesn't this seem to be ridiculous? After all, what does the societal ranking of Naomi and Monica have to do with Olinda?

To provide another example, suppose the societal ranking is Bush ≻ Gore ≻ Nader. The election tallies suggest that if fewer people had liked Nader, then Gore would have beaten Bush. In other words, this phenomenon where what voters think about one candidate can change the outcome for a different pair causes many of our election paradoxes.

To find procedures free from this difficulty, Arrow imposed his IIA condition. This condition requires the societal ranking of a particular pair to depend only on how the voters rank that pair; for that particular ranking, it is irrelevant what the voters think of the other candidates.

To state this in more formal language, let $F$ be the election mapping. For any two alternatives, say $A$ and $B$, suppose that $\mathbf{p}_1$ and $\mathbf{p}_2$ are any two profiles where each voter has identical relative rankings of $A$ and $B$. The condition requires the relative societal ranking of $A$ and $B$ to remain the same for both profiles. That is, the $A$-$B$ relative ranking is the same for $F(\mathbf{p}_1)$ and $F(\mathbf{p}_2)$.

To further illustrate the IIA condition, return to the (page 29) story about hiring one person where $\mathbf{p}_1$ is the above five-voter profile for Mary, Nancy, and Sue. The plurality election ranking, by a 3:2:0 tally, is

Mary ≻ Nancy ≻ Sue.

Suppose, however, that the day before the committee has its final vote, Clark, Elton, and Jeff discover that Sue recently proved an important result. As a result, they change their common ranking to "Sue ≻ Mary ≻ Nancy." With this change, the election ranking becomes

Sue ≻ Nancy ≻ Mary.

The point is that even though each voter keeps the same "Mary-Nancy" ranking, the relative societal ranking of these two candidates is reversed. Therefore, the plurality vote does not satisfy IIA.

Clearly, the plurality vote fails to satisfy the above conditions. But we already know this from the 2000 election. The next step is to determine what procedures do work.

**Theorem 1** (Arrow [2]). *The only procedure which satisfies the above five conditions is a dictatorship. That is, it is the procedure where the societal outcome always agrees with a particular voter's preferences.*

The issue has nothing to do with using a dictatorship as a form of government. Instead, Arrow's result states that whenever we are not subject to

a dictatorship, then at least one of the five specified conditions is not satisfied. Stated in another manner, since these conditions seem to be standard,
the message is to expect election paradoxes.

A pragmatic interpretation of Arrow's result is that for all of the earlier
described procedures — the instant runoff, the Borda Count, the plurality
vote, and on and on — we must anticipate situations much like the 2000
Presidential election where changes in how some voters view one candidate
can reverse the relative ranking of some other two candidates. In other
words, Arrow's result states that the "winner" between the two major candidates might be determined not by what the voters think about the major
candidates, but by what the voters think about someone else, such as Nader.

Sounds discouraging. However, it is not. Instead, as indicated later,
there are explanations of this theorem which allow for more comfortable
conclusions. Also, when a mathematician encounters a result stating that
"all procedures" suffer, the natural instinct is to discover a distinction among
them; for instance, which procedures are "less likely" to suffer these problems? Answers now are known; they are indicated in what follows.

# Chapter 2

# Voter Preferences, or the Procedure?

Who cares about the election procedure? What difference does the choice of weights or the voting method make? Won't the election outcome remain essentially the same with any reasonable approach? Bill Clinton, for instance, failed to receive a majority vote during the 1992 Presidential election. Could George Bush have beaten Clinton with a different election method?

To add some historical suspense, go way back to the closely contested Presidential election of 1860, an election held in a trying tense time in American history just prior to the Civil War. Would Stephen Douglas have beaten Abraham Lincoln had the U.S. used a different election method? Answers for these questions are given later. But, beyond describing what could have happened with specific elections, my goal is to develop a systematic way to analyze all possible differences that can arise among positional elections.

In this chapter, I describe the surprisingly wide assortment of paradoxical outcomes which can occur just by using different positional voting methods. Recall, these methods are defined by a *voting vector* $(w_1, w_2, \ldots, w_n)$, $w_1 > w_n = 0$, and $w_j \geq w_{j+1}$, where ballots are tallied by assigning $w_j$ points to a voter's $j$th ranked candidate, $j = 1, \ldots, n$. For instance, $(6, 5, 0)$ means that ballots are tallied by assigning six points to a voter's top-ranked candidate, five to the second-ranked candidate, and zero to the bottom-ranked one. With this notation, the plurality vote corresponds to $(1, 0, \ldots, 0)$, the antiplurality vote to $(1, 1, \ldots, 1, 0)$, while the Borda Count (BC) is $(n-1, n-2, \ldots, 1, 0)$. If there are five candidate, the BC vector $(4, 3, 2, 1, 0)$ truly is related to the "four-point grading system."

After providing examples to develop intuition about what can happen, general results are stated. Later, in Chapter 6, I indicate that these problems extend beyond voting to plague statistics and other topics.

## 1. Some examples

It is that time of the year to select a speaker for the distinguished *Henri Poinkoff Lecture Series.* After much deliberation, the eleven departmental members on the selection committee settle on three potential speakers, $\{A, B, C\}$. The profile, or list of preferences of the eleven committee members, is as follows:

(8)

| Number | Preferences | Number | Preferences |
|--------|-------------|--------|-------------|
| 3 | $A \succ B \succ C$ | 2 | $B \succ C \succ A$ |
| 2 | $A \succ C \succ B$ | 4 | $C \succ B \succ A$ |

The decision seems clear; the plurality outcome identifies $A$ as the committee's favorite with the plurality ranking of

$$A \succ C \succ B \text{ supported by a } 5 : 4 : 2 \text{ tally.}$$

But one of the committee members has experienced far too many paradoxical election outcomes, so she no longer trusts the plurality vote. When continually pressed to suggest an alternative approach, almost in a fit of frustration she argues that each committee member should vote for two candidates. The committee agrees, but after it does so, they discover that the *antiplurality election outcome*[1] yields the reversed

$$B \succ C \succ A \text{ with the } 9 : 8 : 5 \text{ tally.}$$

Who is the real choice, $A$ or $B$? After much deliberation, the committee decides to vote once more; this time they will use the Borda Count (BC) with its voting vector $(2, 1, 0)$. As one committee member noted, since $(2, 1, 0) = (1, 0, 0) + (1, 1, 0)$, the Borda Count can be viewed as "averaging" what happens with the plurality and antiplurality method. Consequently, the expectation was for this vote to determine between $A$ or $B$. However, the BC outcome is

$$C \succ B \succ A \text{ with the } 12 : 11 : 10 \text{ tally.}$$

What a quandary! The election winner changes with the procedure.

- $A$ wins when they vote for one.
- $B$ wins when they vote for two.
- $C$ wins when they use the Borda Count.

---

[1] Remember, the "anti" modifier refers to the choice of weights, not the coincidence of this example that the election outcomes are reversed.

As this example clearly illustrates, each of these three candidates can be the "winner" by using an appropriate voting procedure. Because the data remains fixed and only the procedure changed, we find that *rather than reflecting the views of the voters, it is entirely possible for an election outcome to more accurately reflect the choice of an election procedure.*

Quite frankly, this behavior, where the outcome and even the winner can switch with a change in the election procedure, is surprisingly common. For instance, consider the following, seemingly innocuous nine-voter profile for the four candidates to be the new Dean for the college.

(9)

| Number | Preference | Number | Preference |
|--------|------------|--------|------------|
| 2 | $A \succ B \succ C \succ D$ | 2 | $C \succ B \succ D \succ A$ |
| 2 | $A \succ D \succ C \succ B$ | 3 | $D \succ B \succ C \succ A$ |

This profile leads to the following troubling behavior.

- Candidate $A$ wins with the plurality vote $(1, 0, 0, 0)$.

- Poor $B$ did not receive a single first-place vote, but she wins when each voter votes for two candidates (i.e., with the voting vector $(1, 1, 0, 0)$).

- When the voters vote for three candidates (with $(1, 1, 1, 0)$), $C$ wins.

- Don't worry about $D$ being left out because she wins with the *Borda Count*; that is, $D$ wins with the voting vector $(3, 2, 1, 0)$.

Again, each of the four candidates can be the "winner" with an appropriate election procedure. So who is the real first choice of these voters to be the new Dean? The message from this example remains the same as the previous one; election outcomes can more accurately reflect the choice of an election procedure rather than the voters' preferences.

These two examples raise the realistic worry that, inadvertently, we may not select whom we really want. With this reality in mind, let me ask: in your last election — maybe it was for a new chair of your department or your social group, or maybe it was to find a candidate for that one tenure-track position — did the election outcome reflect what your *group preferred?* Or did the conclusion more accurately reflect which voting procedure you happened to use?

To show that this problem just gets worse with more candidates, consider the following fourteen-voter profile.

(10)

| Number | Preference | Number | Preference |
|--------|-----------|--------|-----------|
| 3 | $A \succ B \succ C \succ D \succ E$ | 2 | $D \succ C \succ E \succ A \succ B$ |
| 1 | $A \succ C \succ E \succ D \succ B$ | 1 | $E \succ A \succ C \succ D \succ B$ |
| 2 | $A \succ E \succ C \succ D \succ B$ | 3 | $E \succ B \succ D \succ A \succ C$ |
| 2 | $C \succ B \succ D \succ E \succ A$ | | |

The profile has the following behavior:

- $A$ wins when the voters vote for one candidate.

- $B$ wins when the voters vote for two candidates.

- $C$ wins when the voters vote for three candidates.

- $D$ wins when the voters vote for four candidates.

- $E$ wins with the Borda Count with weights $(4, 3, 2, 1, 0)$.

The point is made; with surprisingly few voters, a shockingly large number of election outcomes can arise with changes in how the ballots are tallied. The following result shows that this perverse election phenomenon, where any candidate can win, continues for any number of candidates. This kind of assertion should cause each of us to worry about "our" election procedure.

**Theorem 2** (Saari [**46**]). *For $N \geq 3$ candidates $\{c_1, c_2, \ldots, c_N\}$, there exist profiles — choices of how the voters rank the candidates — so that $c_j$ wins when the voters vote for $j$ candidates, $j = 1, \ldots, N-1$, and then $c_N$ is the Borda Count winner.*

Incidentally, when proving results such as the above, I have not tried to determine the minimal number of voters required for the various conclusions. Based on the above examples, however, it is reasonable to conjecture that the number of voters can be surprisingly small. But rather than worrying about the number of voters, my main message is intentionally directed toward the selection of a procedure. Does the choice of an election procedure matter? It surely does.

**1.1. How bad can it get?** The above examples identify only who is the "winner." It is worth wondering how bad the situation can be when the full rankings are considered. The answer is that it can be bad, quite bad. To illustrate, I already showed for the *Poinkoff Lecture Series* example (page 34) that this Eq. 8 eleven-voter profile allows three different "winners." A more careful examination, however, proves that this example allows *seven* different election rankings; the different rankings emerge as the choice of the positional election procedure changes.

(11)

| Procedure | Ranking | Procedure | Ranking |
|-----------|---------|-----------|---------|
| $(1,0,0)$ | $A \succ C \succ B$ | $(2,1,0)$ | $C \succ B \succ A$ |
| $(4,1,0)$ | $A \approx C \succ B$ | $(3,2,0)$ | $B \approx C \succ A$ |
| $(7,2,0)$ | $C \succ A \succ B$ | $(1,1,0)$ | $B \succ C \succ A$ |
| $(7,3,0)$ | $C \succ A \approx B$ | | |

Adding to the societal confusion of trying to meet the wishes of these voters is that these election rankings range from the plurality ranking of $A \succ C \succ B$ all the way to the directly opposite election ranking of $B \succ C \succ A$. With this wide variance in election outcomes, it is difficult to venture even a guess about which ranking best reflects the voters' wishes.

The natural question, suggested by this example, is to understand, in general, how varied election outcomes can be. The answer follows.

**Theorem 3** (Saari [**46**]). *Suppose there are $N \geq 2$ candidates. For any $k$ satisfying[2] $1 \leq k \leq N! - (N-1)!$, a profile can be found where there are precisely $k$ strict positional election outcomes; the different election rankings arise as the choice of the positional election procedure changes. It is impossible to find a profile with more than $N! - (N-1)!$ strict positional election rankings.*

In other words, there are three-candidate examples with as many as $3! - 2! = (3 \times 2 \times 1) - (2 \times 1) = 4$ different strict election outcomes. Such an example is the Poinkoff Lecture Series (Eq. 8) profile. This result also means that there exist four-candidate profiles allowing $4! - 3! = 24 - 6 = 18$ different strict election outcomes. Adding to the discouraging news of this theorem is that the conclusion cannot be dismissed by conjecturing that it holds only for complicated, highly unlikely examples. Instead, the supporting profile may be reasonably simple; indeed, an example with this behavior is the innocuous appearing Eq. 9 profile for the Dean selection.

The factorial expression allows the number of disparate outcomes to radically increase with the number of candidates. Already for $N = 5$ candidates, this theorem ensures the existence of profiles which allow $5! - 4! = 120 - 24 = 96$ different strict election rankings. Such a profile need not be outrageous; Eq. 10 is a fourteen-voter example.

To provide a sense about how fast the number of strict different positional election outcomes coming from a single profile — how the numbers of outcomes can jump into the millions and billions and even trillions with more candidates — the following table computes some of the values. (In

---

[2]This standard factorial notation means $N! = N \times (N-1) \times \cdots \times 2 \times 1$. So $3! = 3 \times 2 \times 1 = 6$ and $4! = 4 \times 3 \times 2 \times 1 = 24$.

this table, $N$ is the number of candidates, and the "Number" is the number of possible strict election rankings.)

| N | Number | N | Number |
|---|--------|---|--------|
| 2 | 1 | 9 | $322,560$ |
| 3 | 4 | 10 | $3,265,920$ |
| 4 | 18 | 11 | $36,288,000$ |
| 5 | 96 | 12 | $439,084,800$ |
| 6 | 600 | 13 | $5,748,019,200$ |
| 7 | 4320 | 14 | $80,951,270,400$ |
| 8 | $35,280$ | 15 | $1,219,496,076,800$ |

Already with only ten candidates ($N = 10$) — and this is about the number of candidates who started in the Republican presidential primary during the 1996 and 2000 election seasons, or the number of candidates for the President of France — millions of strict election rankings can result for the same ballots just by changing the positional election procedure. The voters do not change their minds; all these different outcomes arise by using different tallying methods. So who is the real choice of the voters? In some of the crowded 2000 Republican primaries, would John McCain have done better with a different voting method? How about Robert Dole in the 1996 New Hampshire Republican primary; would he have beaten Pat Buchanan with a different method? (Yes.) With a different procedure, could Gore have won in 2000? (Absolutely.)

Once there are 13 candidates, the number of possible election rankings, from the same data, jumps into the billions, and with only 15 candidates the number escalates to the trillions. Now imagine what can happen with 20 candidates — as is the case with the weekly ranking of collegiate football teams. Here the number of strict possible rankings for a fixed profile reaches the astronomical value of more than $2 \times 10^{18}$ — this number has the value 2 followed by 18 zeros. Examples of 25 candidates, as true for the weekly ranking of collegiate basketball teams, allow the number of possible rankings to range as high as $1.5 \times 10^{25}$. It is impossible to even count to this number, even if counting as fast as possible and starting at the "Big Bang."

While astonishingly large numbers of different rankings can occur, it is worth wondering whether they can be widely varied. As the next result asserts, they can be surprisingly contradictory.

**Theorem 4** (Saari [**46, 57**]). *For $N \geq 4$ candidates, there exist a profile where, with appropriate choices of positional election procedures, each candidate is listed in first, second, ... , and in last place.*

So, for the candidates $\{A, B, C, D\}$, there are profiles where $A$ is in first place with some procedures, in second place with others, in third place with another set of methods, and finally bottom ranked with other procedures. But $A$ is not the only candidate suffering changeable fortunes; the same conclusion holds for *all four candidates.* Candidates $B$, and $C$, and $D$ all suffer the same variable fate when different voting methods are used.

By the way, in these statements the wording "a profile" is used only for purposes of clarity of exposition. In fact, there are many — actually, an infinite number — of such profiles; i.e., using a natural topology over profiles, there are open sets of profiles with this property.

**1.2. How likely is it?** One might hope to be able to dismiss these difficulties as mere anomalies characterized by concocted examples. Perhaps they can be ignored as being highly unlikely to occur. Unfortunately, this is not the case; differences in election outcomes are more likely to occur than not.

Using fairly conservative assumptions about the distribution of profiles, it turns out that, with three candidates, almost 70% of the profiles allow the election ranking to change with a change in the tallying procedure. If we include paradoxical outcomes caused by conflicts with pairwise rankings, then *over three-fourths of the profiles lead to some unexpected outcome.* The message is to expect the unexpected with elections.

**Theorem 5** (Saari and Tataru [**64**]). *Suppose the probability distribution for the profiles satisfies standard assumptions allowing the use of the central limit theorem.*[3] *The limiting probability as the number of voters increases (namely, as the number of voters approaches infinity) that the profile permits precisely $k$ different outcomes as the* $\mathbf{w}_s$ *choice varies is zero if $k$ is an even integer, and*

| $k$ | *Probability* | $k$ | *Probability* |
|---|---|---|---|
| 1 | 0.31 | 3 | 0.44 |
| 5 | 0.19 | 7 | 0.06 |

The "zero probability" assertion for even values of $k$ seems peculiar. It arises because these $k$ values require the profile to have an unlikely tied plurality or antiplurality election outcome.[4] The proof of this theorem heavily relies on the analytic-geometric results developed by Schläfli [**69**]; also see Coxeter [**17**]. For our purposes, it suffices to say that the proof computes answers with the "central limit theorem" in a five-dimensional space. This "central limit theorem" is a "bell-shaped curve" assertion about the distribution of the voters' preferences. A crucial part of the analysis, which

---

[3]The distribution of voter choices is asymptotically independent with an asymptotic common variance and where the asymptotic mean has an equal distribution of voters of each type.

[4]To see why this is the case, after the procedure line is introduced later in this chapter, use it to determine all possible situations with an even number of rankings. It quickly becomes apparent that this situation arises if and only if one of the endpoints is on a line indicating a tied outcome.

determines what needs to be computed, uses the "procedure line" which is introduced later in this chapter.

To explain the "five dimensions," there are $3! = 6$ ways to rank the candidates, so profiles naturally reside in a six-dimensional space. A normalization drops a dimension to reduce the analysis to five dimensions. With three candidates, the analysis is complicated enough, but with more candidates, the dimensions jump significantly. For instance, with four candidates, the computations reside in a $4! - 1 = 24 - 1 = 23$-dimensional space. Then, for five candidates, the computations leap into a 119-dimensional space.

I mention these growing dimensions only to explain why I do not report results for more candidates. After all, one might suspect, and it is true, that Schläfli's results could be used to determine what happens with any number of candidates. But I have not attempted to do so, and neither has anyone else. The obvious reason for this reluctance is that the computations would involve the many technical details which are associated with a high-dimensional space. The analysis would require inventing a complicated notation just to recognize which dimension is being used at what stage, so it would try the patience of someone much more tolerant than I am.

On the other hand, another approach (described in Chapter 5) shows that the likelihood for paradoxical behavior radically increases with the number of alternatives. With about six candidates, for instance, it is reasonable to expect that more than 96% of the profiles allow the election rankings to change with the procedure. In other words, fully expect this troubling behavior, a behavior which should instill serious doubt about any election. Not only are these election ranking difficulties worrisome, but they also are surprisingly and uncomfortably likely. This statement underscores the earlier warning that we should worry about most election outcomes.

## 2. Representation triangle and profiles

As these results demonstrate, election rankings can wildly vary with changes in the tallying method. But why? Why do all of these conflicting results occur? The explanation offered here uses some elementary geometry.

**2.1. A geometric representation of profiles.** My discussion describing the source of paradoxes will require the reader to compute some election tallies. But let's face it; *nobody* enjoys tallying ballots. For instance, I expect that the reader fully accepted my word about the tallies for the earlier examples without really checking them.

What makes the tallying processes so irritating is the tedious effort required to sift the data to determine how many voters ranked a certain candidate first, then second, and so forth. This is boring! To avoid this time-consuming annoyance, I developed a convenient, geometric way to represent profiles. One value of this representation is that it simplifies the tallying of ballots for positional procedures.

My approach uses an equilateral simplex (Saari [**49**]). For three candidates, this simplex becomes the familiar equilateral triangle. To define "ranking regions," assign each candidate a unique vertex; in Fig. 2.1a, for instance, candidate $A$ is assigned the vertex in the lower left corner. Next, assign a point in the triangle a ranking according to its distance to each vertex where, as with love, "closer is better." Of course, there are lines of points which are equal distance from a pair of vertices; they define regions of "tied" or "indifferent" outcomes.

In this manner, the assignment process divides the representation triangle into the six smaller triangular regions of Fig. 2.1a. For instance, as the Fig. 2.1a region with a "4" is closest to the $C$ vertex, next closest to the $B$ vertex, and most distant from the $A$ vertex, all points in this triangular region share the ordinal ranking $C \succ B \succ A$. To geometrically represent a profile, list the number of voters with a particular ranking in the corresponding ranking region. So, the "4" in the $C \succ B \succ A$ region means that four voters have these preferences. In this manner, the Fig. 2.1a profile is the earlier Table 8 profile.

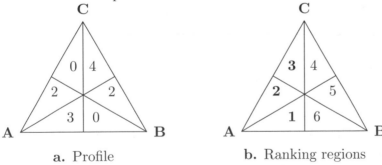

**a.** Profile       **b.** Ranking regions

**Fig. 2.1.** Profiles

While I prefer the triangular profile representation, I also use a vector description to save considerable space. But a vector description requires ordering the rankings; my preferred ordering is indicated by the numbers in the Fig. 2.1b ranking regions. Thus, the numbers in Fig. 2.1b are *type numbers*; this is *not* a profile.[5] For instance, since "3" is in the $C \succ A \succ B$

---

[5]To avoid confusion, this is the *only figure* where the numbers do not represent a profile.

region, this is a "type-three ranking." More generally,

(12)

| Ranking | Type Number | Ranking | Type Number |
|---------|-------------|---------|-------------|
| $A \succ B \succ C$ | 1 | $C \succ B \succ A$ | 4 |
| $A \succ C \succ B$ | 2 | $B \succ C \succ A$ | 5 |
| $C \succ A \succ B$ | 3 | $B \succ A \succ C$ | 6 |

Voter types

With these labels, $\mathbf{p} = (p_1, \ldots, p_6)$ becomes a profile where $p_j$ is the number of voters with the $j$th ranking. The Fig. 2.1a profile, for instance, has the vector representation $\mathbf{p} = (3, 2, 0, 4, 2, 0)$. These numbers start from the lower left region and go clockwise around the triangle.

**2.2. Computing election tallies.** I now exploit the geometry to tally ballots. The approach is illustrated by using the Fig. 2.1a profile which, for convenience, is reproduced in Fig. 2.2a.

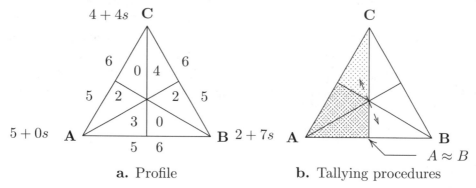

a. Profile          b. Tallying procedures

**Fig. 2.2.** Profile and tallies

To use the geometry to facilitate the computation of the pairwise outcomes, notice that all voters preferring $A$ to $B$ are listed to the left of the vertical line (representing a $A \approx B$ tie). Thus, $A$'s pairwise tally of 5 is the sum of the terms which would be placed in the three shaded regions of Fig. 2.2b; $B$'s tally of 6 for the Fig. 2.2a profile is the sum of the values to the right of the vertical line.

All pairwise tallies ($B \succ A$ by 6:5, $C \succ A$ by 6:5 and $C \succ B$ by 6:5) are similarly computed relative to the appropriate indifference line; they are listed under the proper Fig. 2.2a edges. To "see" this computation for $B$ and $C$, turn this book so that the triangle edge connecting $B$ and $C$ is horizontal. As this twist places the $B \approx C$ indifference line in a vertical position, the same description holds. This example also allows terminology to be introduced; because $C$ beats all other candidates in pairwise elections,

$C$ is called the *Condorcet winner*. Since $A$ loses to everyone, she is the *Condorcet loser*.

To compute the positional outcomes, notice that as $A$'s plurality tally is the number of voters who have $A$ top ranked, it is the sum of terms which would be in the two heavily shaded Fig. 2.2b regions with $A$ as a vertex. For the Fig. 2.2a profile, for instance, the plurality tallies of $A$, $B$, and $C$ are, respectively, 5, 2, 4.

What hinders computing all positional outcomes is that there are too many procedures. On the other hand, many of these methods are essentially the same. For instance, while the tallies would be drastically inflated should each vote in a plurality election be assigned 50 points (using $(50, 0, 0)$), rather than one (using $(1, 0, 0)$), both approaches have the same election ranking. More generally, an election *ranking* remains the same whether the ballots are tallied with $(w_1, w_2, \ldots, 0)$ or with $(\lambda w_1, \lambda w_2, \ldots, \lambda 0)$ where $\lambda > 0$ is a fixed scalar. This fact suggests culling the procedures by scaling the weights of the positional methods.

The normalization used here replaces $(w_1, w_2, \ldots, 0)$ by letting $\lambda = 1/w_1$. So, for three candidates, instead of $(w_1, w_2, 0)$, use $(\frac{w_1}{w_1}, \frac{w_2}{w_1}, 0)$ to create a *normalized voting vector* of the form $\mathbf{w}_s = (1, s, 0)$ where, since $w_1 \geq w_2$, we have that $0 \leq s = \frac{w_2}{w_1} \leq 1$. To illustrate, if the ballots for your next election are tallied by using $(6, 5, 0)$ (that is, assign six, five, and zero points, respectively, to a voter's first, second, and third ranked candidate), the normalized form is $\mathbf{w}_{5/6} = (\frac{6}{6}, \frac{5}{6}, 0)$. The Borda Count, with its usual $(2, 1, 0)$ representation, becomes $\mathbf{w}_{1/2} = (1, \frac{1}{2}, 0)$.

This normalization allows us to discover what happens with all possible three-candidate positional methods just by computing all $\mathbf{w}_s = (1, s, 0)$ tallies. We already have seen how the geometry helps compute outcomes with $s = 0$ — this is the plurality vote. The computation of all other $\mathbf{w}_s$ outcomes is equally easy. For instance, $A$'s $\mathbf{w}_s$ tally is the number of voters who have her top ranked — this is $A$'s plurality vote — plus $s$ times the number of voters who have $A$ second ranked. According to the geometry, these are the two small triangular regions with an edge on the heavily shaded regions; they are the two Fig. 2.2b regions with arrows.

So, using Fig. 2.2b, $A$'s $\mathbf{w}_s$ tally is the sum of terms in the heavily shaded region (the plurality vote) plus $s\times$ [sum of terms in two regions indicated by the arrows.] For the Fig. 2.2a profile, this construction means that $A$'s $\mathbf{w}_s$ vote is $5 + 0s$ while $B$'s is $2 + 7s$ and $C$'s is $4 + 4s$. These tallies are listed near the respective vertex. By having the $\mathbf{w}_s$ tallies, elementary algebra determines which procedures define which rankings. Indeed, this is how Table 11 was determined for the Eq. 8 profile.

**2.3. Creating "paradoxes".** This geometric representation of profiles helps explain why we should expect different procedures to generate different election outcomes. Stated simply and bluntly, different methods use different information about the voters' preferences.

To illustrate, the Fig. 2.3a profile $\mathbf{p} = (2, 6, 0, 5, 0, 7)$ has the same $A \succ B \succ C$ ranking for all $\mathbf{w}_s$-positional methods. So adjust this profile to create an example with the same plurality ranking and tallies, but some conflict with other $\mathbf{w}_s$-election rankings. To specify a challenge, design an example where some positional methods have the directly opposing $C \succ B \succ A$ ranking.

To keep the same plurality tallies, require all voters to keep the same candidate top ranked. So, when moving voter preferences to create a new profile, only move them between the two regions which share the same vertex. For instance, eight voters have $A$ top ranked, so if these preferences are changed, keep them in the two regions that have $A$ as a vertex.

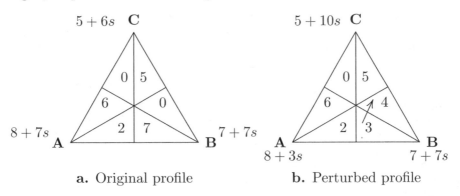

**a.** Original profile           **b.** Perturbed profile

**Fig. 2.3.** Creating examples

To create the desired example, move preferences to enhance $B$'s and $C$'s standings with $\mathbf{w}_s$-procedures; this requires more voters to have $B$ and $C$ second ranked, or not as many to have $A$ second ranked. Such changes do not affect the information used by the plurality method, but they change the information used by the other procedures.

As indicated in Fig. 2.3b, this goal is easy to accomplish; just move some voter preferences out of the regions where $A$ is second ranked. For instance, by persuading four of the seven voters who have $B$ top ranked about the virtues of $C$, they switch their preferences to make her their second choice. This defines the Fig. 2.3b profile $\mathbf{p} = (2, 6, 0, 5, 4, 3)$ (where the arrow indicates the change) which, as illustrated by the tallies, has the desired properties. (For instance, try $s = 1$ with both profiles to see how radically the outcome changes.) Other examples, where, say, $B$ dominates are equally easy to design. In fact, the intuition gained by experimenting with this simple exercise supports the earlier assertion (see Theorem 5) warning us to expect that most profiles will provide different election rankings when different procedures are used.

## 3. Procedure lines and elections

Now that we have a geometric way to view the profiles, we need a geometric representation for the election outcomes. A goal in doing so is to develop intuition about the source of my earlier assertions stating that election outcomes can radically differ when different tallying methods are used. Even more, this geometric approach allows us to characterize all possible paradoxes, all possible arrangements of elections rankings, that ever could occur with positional methods.

First, express each candidate's election tally as a fraction of the total tally. For instance, in a 10,000 voter election, if Alicia, Brenda, and Corrie receive, respectively, 2000, 5000, and 3000 votes, then they receive, respectively, $\frac{2000}{10,000}, \frac{5000}{10,000}$, and $\frac{3000}{10,000}$ of the total vote. This is nothing new; it just mimics the evening news reports that "Brenda received half of the vote, while Alicia and and Corrie received, respectively, a fifth and three-tenths."

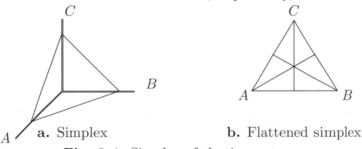

**a.** Simplex        **b.** Flattened simplex

**Fig. 2.4.** Simplex of election outcomes

Changing the names to $A$, $B$, and $C$, this $(\frac{1}{5}, \frac{1}{2}, \frac{3}{10})$ election outcome can be plotted in three space by letting values along the $x$, $y$, and $z$ axis represent, respectively, the votes of candidates $A$, $B$, and $C$. More generally for candidates $\{A, B, C\}$, the fractional tallies are given by

$$\{\mathbf{q} = (q_A, q_B, q_C) \,|\, q_j \geq 0, \ q_A + q_B + q_C = 1\}$$

where $q_j$ is the fraction of the total tally won by the indicated candidate. Thus, $\mathbf{q}$ not only is a point in three-dimensional Euclidean space, it is on the unit simplex — where the sum of the values equals one as represented in Fig. 2.4a — in the positive orthant. The Fig. 2.6b triangle suppresses the coordinate axes and flattens the equilateral triangle.

In the obvious way, the normalized tally $\mathbf{q} = (q_A, q_B, q_C)$ defines the election ranking. For instance, since $B$ received the largest vote in our example, $\mathbf{q}$ is closer to the $B$ vertex. More generally, the closer $\mathbf{q}$ is to a particular vertex, the better that candidate did in the election. (This "closer is better" relationship should sound familiar.) The line defined by $q_A = q_B$ — the vertical line in the triangle on the right in Fig. 2.4 — represents the tallies with a tie vote between these two candidates. The three lines of tied tallies divide the triangle precisely in the manner given in Fig. 2.1, except that now the triangle represents election tallies rather than profiles.

**3.1. Procedure line.** We now are just about ready to characterize everything that can happen. To do so, we need to represent a $\mathbf{w}_s$ election tally as a point in the unit simplex. This is easy to do; just divide each candidate's tally by the total tally. If Allison, Bertha, and Constance received, respectively, 300, 500, 200 points in an election (so the sum of points is 1,000), the normalized tallies would be $(\frac{300}{1000}, \frac{500}{1000}, \frac{200}{1000})$. Again, this is the newscast information that "Bertha received half of the votes, while ... "

To use a more general situation, suppose a profile has the $\mathbf{w}_s$ tallies of $(8 + 3s, 7 + 7s, 5 + 10s)$. (These values come from Fig. 2.3b.) The tallies define, after dividing by the total tally of $20(1 + s)$, the point

$$\mathbf{q}_s = \frac{1}{20(1 + s)}(8 + 3s, 7 + 7s, 5 + 10s).$$

With algebraic manipulations, this expression becomes

(13)     $\mathbf{q}_s = (1 - 2t)(\frac{8}{20}, \frac{7}{20}, \frac{5}{20}) + 2t(\frac{11}{40}, \frac{14}{40}, \frac{15}{40})$,     where $t = \frac{s}{1 + s}$.

This Eq. 13 expression shows that $\mathbf{q}_s$, the $\mathbf{w}_s$ normalized election tally, is a point on a line segment where the endpoints are the profile's normalized plurality and antiplurality outcomes. What makes this comment important is that a similar expression always occurs. Namely, if $\mathbf{q}_s$ represents the normalized tally of a $\mathbf{w}_s$ election, then

(14)                         $\mathbf{q}_s = (1 - 2t)\mathbf{q}_0 + 2t\mathbf{q}_1, \quad t = \frac{s}{1 + s}.$

I call this line of election outcomes the *"procedure line."*

A way to think of this procedure line is to take a rubber band and identify the endpoints as the "plurality" and "antiplurality" ends. Next, stretch the rubber band and place it on the triangle; in doing so, anchor its endpoints on the plotted normalized plurality and antiplurality points.

Any point on the stretched rubber band is an election outcome for some positional method. The outcome for a specific method, say the Borda Count, is determined by its "$t$" value. To illustrate, since the Borda Count is defined by $s = \frac{1}{2}$, the Eq. 14 expression for $t$ means that the BC value is $t = \frac{1}{2}/(1 + \frac{1}{2}) = \frac{2}{3}$. So, mark the unstretched rubber band at the point two-thirds of the way from the plurality end to the antiplurality end. Where that mark ends up when the stretched band is placed on the triangle is the normalized Borda election tally.

The procedure line makes it easy to identify all possible positional election outcomes for a given profile. As suggested with the rubber band analogy, first plot the profile's normalized plurality and antiplurality election outcomes. Each point on the line connecting these points uniquely represents a particular $\mathbf{w}_s$ election tally.

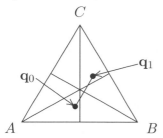

**Fig. 2.5.** Procedure line

Figure 2.5 depicts the procedure line for the tallies we have been using from the Fig. 2.3b profile $\mathbf{p} = (2, 6, 0, 5, 4, 3)$. The $\mathbf{q}_0$ point, with a $A \succ B \succ C$ election ranking, is the profile's normalized plurality outcome. The other endpoint, denoted by $\mathbf{q}_1$, is the normalized antiplurality outcome when voters "vote for two candidates." What is important is the connecting line. *Each point on this line is the profile's election outcome for some positional method!* Because this line crosses *seven ranking regions* (four are open triangles representing strict election outcomes and three are lines representing a tie), this profile allows the seven election rankings

$$A \succ B \succ C, \quad A \approx B \succ C, \quad B \succ A \succ C, \quad B \succ A \approx C,$$
$$B \succ C \succ A, \quad B \approx C \succ A, \quad C \succ B \succ A.$$

To put some emotion into these rankings, if the profile represents the differing opinions in your organization, then the exact election outcome dictating the future of your group is determined by the voting method your group uses. This profile allows each candidate to be the "winner" with an appropriate way to tally the ballots, so who will guide your group?

It is natural to pause and wonder where does all of this leave us. Quite frankly, it warns us to expect an electoral mess. This mathematical structure strongly underscores the reality that an election outcome can more accurately reflect which election procedure was used rather than what the voters believe. It alerts us to the danger that if we do not use the "correct" voting method, we run the serious risk of inadvertently choosing badly.

**3.2. Could Clinton have lost in 1992?** The 2000 election season will be cited for years as an example of a controversial election. But another controversial outcome was the 1992 Clinton - Bush - Perot election where Bill Clinton won with only about 43% of the popular vote to Bush's 37.4%.

In the first chapter, the reader was cautioned to worry about any election involving three or more candidates where the winner failed to receive a majority of the vote. To take this advice seriously, we should wonder whether the senior George Bush could have been re-elected to the presidency in 1992 had a different voting procedure been used. How about Ross Perot? Could he have been elected with some  method?

These kinds of questions are occasionally described in the political science literature. But the usual published paper is limited to discussing what would have happened if the voters had used "this procedure," or "that procedure." While these conclusions might be interesting, they most surely do not answer the central question. It remains unknown what might have happened if the voters had used one of an infinite number of other approaches. What might have happened with them?

Alex Tabarrok, who was an economist at Ball State University at the time, used my "procedure line" to address this more general question [78]. He realized that by using this geometric approach, rather than just discovering what would happen with one or two standard methods, he could determine *all possible positional outcomes* for the 1992 election just by plotting the normalized plurality and antiplurality tallies. Then, by connecting these points with a straight line — or stretching a rubber band between them — he could geometrically determine whether any procedure could have elected someone other than Clinton.

Remember, to use this approach, Tabarrok needed to know more than the press reports about how the Perot voters would split in their preferences; we already knew that these Perot voters split somewhat equally between ranking Bush and Clinton in second place. To use the procedure line, Tabarrok also needed to know how the Clinton voters would have split between Bush and Perot and how the Bush voters would have split between Clinton and Perot. This extra, more refined information is required to determine the antiplurality — the "vote for two" — outcome. Fortunately, Tabarrok was able to obtain the data.

His results proved that the procedure line is strictly within the

"Clinton ≻ Bush ≻ Perot" ranking region.

This means that no matter what positional procedure would have been used in this election, Clinton would have won, Bush would have been second, and Perot always would be last. Tabarrok also showed that the same ranking would apply with pairwise "head-to-head" elections. This means, for instance, that if a runoff had been used, or if we had used some other procedure combining pairwise and positional outcomes, Clinton still would have been victorious. In other words, although Clinton won the 1992 election with only about 43% of the popular vote, a more careful analysis proves that, in fact, he enjoyed a "strong" victory.

But the question remains. Are there other procedures where, say, Perot could have won the election? Surprisingly, there are; as described later in this chapter, Tabarrok found voting methods which would have allowed *any* of the three candidates — Bush, Clinton, or Perot — to win the election depending on how voters decided to use them. Moreover, these procedures which would permit "anyone to win" are not wild methods concocted to demonstrate perverse results; they are voting approaches that have been used in actual elections.

The same analysis applies to the 2000 election. As far as the popular vote is concerned, Gore was the plurality winner. To design a procedure line, we need to determine the "vote for two" election outcome. While I do not have reliable data at the time of this writing, from press reports about how the Nader votes would have split,[6] it appears that the procedure line, for the *popular vote*, would have the "Gore $\succ$ Bush $\succ$ Nader" ranking for all positional procedures.

The critical election in Florida, on the other hand, would allow fascinating, mixed results. As the whole world knows, the plurality vote gave George W. Bush a narrow victory. According to press reports about how the Nader vote would have split, it is clear that Gore would have won with many other choices of positional methods. In fact, a conservative use of available data suggests that Gore would have won in Florida with most positional methods including the Borda Count.

There remains an interesting question. Was the Florida election anxiety sufficiently contentious so that most George W. Bush voters and most Al Gore voters would rank Nader in second place? I doubt this. However, and this is just malicious speculation, if this could have been the case, then Nader would have been the "vote for two" winner in Florida. In turn, by stretching that "rubber band," it follows that the subsequent position of the procedure line would indicate that *any of the three candidates could have won in Florida with an appropriate voting method.* What a mess! If Nader had won, the decision would have been made by the House of Representatives. Later I describe other consequences of this speculation to show that other methods would create an even more chaotic state of affairs.

---

[6] But the most fascinating and important aspect, which is part of the analysis, is whom the Bush and Gore voters would have had in second place; this is not clear.

**3.3. Positioning the position line.** How widely varied can the three-candidate positional outcomes be? Is it possible to find all possible "paradoxes?" To rephrase this question, can we determine all possible ways election outcomes can change as the procedure changes?

A natural way to tackle this issue is to construct many profiles and then determine the associated position of the procedure line. The different positions of the procedure line would then indicate how varied the election outcomes can be. However, this is difficult work; the associated combinatorics involved with constructing profiles guarantees that such an approach would involve considerable effort with only limited conclusions.

A more serious limitation is that the analysis never is finished. Although this approach would create a non-ending supply of research problems for students, it also leaves us with an unsatisfying sense of incompleteness. This is because, even after billions upon billions of examples are generated and carefully analyzed, some spoil sport could legitimately ask, "That's nice. But have you found everything? Maybe just one more example will demonstrate something radically different." To address these concerns, to try to find a sense of closure, we need to devise an easier, more encompassing approach.

A way to get around this problem is to emphasize the procedure line. After all, since we are primarily interested in understanding all ways this procedure line can be positioned, the profile merely serves to verify that, yes, some profile allows the procedure line to be placed in such a fashion. This suggests solving the inverse problem:

> Find all ways to position a line segment in the triangle so that
> this positioning is the procedure line for some profile.

The procedure line is defined by its endpoints, so this task involves finding all admissible pairs of $\mathbf{q}_0$ and $\mathbf{q}_1$ (the normalized plurality and antiplurality outcomes) which are defined by a profile. Let me start by identifying obvious constraints that $\mathbf{q}_0$ and $\mathbf{q}_1$ always must satisfy.

Quite obviously, a candidate's antiplurality tally cannot be less than her plurality tally. This is because her antiplurality tally equals the number of voters who have her top ranked — her plurality tally — *plus* the number of voters who have her second ranked. On the other hand, because each voter's *first- and second-* ranked candidates get a vote, the sum of antiplurality votes is twice that of the plurality vote. Thus, the antiplurality normalization uses a denominator twice as large as that for the plurality denominator. In other words, these natural constraints mean that

> each $\mathbf{q}_1$ component is no less than half the corresponding $\mathbf{q}_0$
> component.

For instance, $\mathbf{q}_1 = (\frac{1}{2}, \frac{1}{3}, \frac{1}{6})$ satisfies this condition with $\mathbf{q}_0 = (\frac{1}{3}, \frac{1}{3}, \frac{1}{3})$ because $A$'s and $B$'s normalized antiplurality tallies are greater than half of their normalized plural tallies, while $C$'s normalized antiplurality tally $(\frac{1}{6})$ is precisely half of her normalized plurality tally $(\frac{1}{3}$; this equality indicates that nobody had $C$ second-ranked). However, the above normalized $\mathbf{q}_1$ is *not* compatible with $\mathbf{q}_0' = (\frac{1}{3} - \frac{1}{100}, \frac{1}{3}, \frac{1}{3} + \frac{1}{100})$ because $C$'s tallies violate the above constraint with $\frac{1}{6} < \frac{1}{2}[\frac{1}{3} + \frac{1}{100}]$.

A second obvious constraint comes from the maximum number of votes a candidate can receive. In a plurality vote, a candidate can receive no votes, or she could even receive all of them. Thus, other than specifying that the value is between zero and unity, there is no constraint on the normalized value of a component of the plurality vote.

The situation changes with the "vote for two" procedure. Even if everyone votes for one candidate, say Helvi, they also have to vote for someone else. This means that no candidate receives more than half of all votes cast. When the tallies are normalized, this means that

each $\mathbf{q}_1$ component is bounded above by $\frac{1}{2}$.

Somewhat surprisingly, these are the only two constraints which need to be imposed on $\mathbf{q}_0$ and $\mathbf{q}_1$.[7] Therefore, for any line segment drawn in the triangle which satisfies these conditions, a profile exists which has that line segment as a procedure line. Notice, these constraints just mean that after the plurality point $\mathbf{q}_0$ is placed anywhere one wishes in the triangle,

- the antiplurality $\mathbf{q}_1$ point must be in the smaller triangle formed by connecting the three midpoints of the edges and

- $\mathbf{q}_1$ cannot be too much closer to any edge of the full triangle than $\mathbf{q}_0$.

This highly relaxed constraint, depicted in Fig. 2.6, allows almost anything to happen!

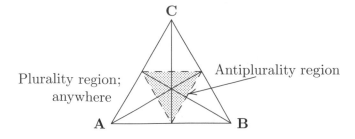

**Fig. 2.6.** Restrictions on procedure line

---

[7]Well, there is another condition; the $\mathbf{q}_0$ and $\mathbf{q}_1$ components must be fractions.

Finding new results about voting procedures now resembles one of those child's games of exploring how a stick can be placed on a figure. For voting, it follows that just about any way to place a line on the triangle (subject to the two simple rules) identifies an allowable combination of positional election outcomes. The following provides a sample of the possible "paradoxes."

- By selecting $\mathbf{q}_0 = \mathbf{q}_1$, the procedure line degenerates into a point. This means that *profiles can be found where all positional methods share the same normalized election tally.* For instance, there is a profile where all $\mathbf{w}_s$ methods have the same $(\frac{4}{9}, \frac{3}{9}, \frac{2}{9})$ normalized tally. Again, supporting profiles need not be overly complicated; the profile $\mathbf{p} = (2, 2, 1, 1, 0, 3)$ defines this point.

- Draw a line passing through the baricentric point which represents a complete $A \approx B \approx C$ tie. It follows that *there exists a profile with precisely three election outcomes. One is the complete tie; the other two have opposite election rankings.*

- For any $k$ between 1 and 4, a line can be drawn which passes through precisely $k$ small triangles. This proves the three-candidate case of Theorem 3. Namely, *for any integer $k$, $1 \leq k \leq 4$, there is a profile allowing precisely $k$ different election outcomes as the election procedure changes.*

  If we include tie rankings, then, because a line can be drawn to pass through precisely $j$ ranking regions, where $1 \leq j \leq 7$, it follows that there is a profile with precisely $j$ different positional rankings.

- If a profile allows an even number of election rankings, then an end of the procedure line must be on a line indicating indifference. Thus, if $j$ is an even integer, either the plurality or the antiplurality outcome has a tie.

- A line can be drawn to pass through regions where each candidate is bottom ranked, or to pass through regions where each candidate is top ranked. This means that *there are profiles where, with appropriate positional methods, each candidate is bottom ranked, and there are other profiles where, with appropriate positional methods, each candidate is top ranked.*

- Each $\mathbf{w}_s$ procedure is a specified point on the procedure line. But, by placing the procedure line close enough to the baricentric point, the line can be positioned so that any two specified points are in different specified ranking regions. Consequently, *it is possible to specify rankings for any two different positional procedures, and there exists a profile so that the election outcome is as specified.*

While the above only samples what can happen, it underscores the reality that election outcomes can be varied depending on the choice of the procedure. The main message is to worry about how elections are conducted; the choice matters.

## 4. Approval or Cumulative voting?

A person first learning about this area may find it disturbing to discover how varied the election outcomes for a fixed profile can be. But if this lack of decisiveness, this sense of randomness causes a headache, let me escalate the problem into a full blown migraine. Some methods, including the "divide ten points," create much worse problems.

Approval Voting (AV) has been adopted by several professional societies, including one decision science and two of the main American mathematical societies. As such, and because I belong to all three organizations, it is worth comparing a profile's positional and AV outcomes. To do so with an actual election, I use the data coming from the 1999 AV election for a new president of the Society for Social Choice & Welfare (SC&W).

**4.1. Social Choice & Welfare election.** To set the stage, all three SC&W candidates, identified as $A$, $B$, $C$, were popular and highly regarded. Thus, the voters were treated to a rare event — a closely contested election for a professional society. Thanks to the initiative of Steven Brams, SC&W converted this Approval Voting election into a "voting theory" testing ground. This means that, in addition to voting, each voter was asked to rank the three candidates. In this manner, by having the actual Fig. 2.7a profile, the AV outcome could be analyzed with *actual data* rather than the dubious standard approach which uses speculative reconstructions of what the data *might* have been.

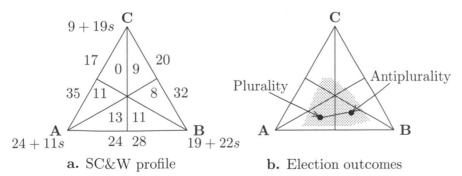

**a.** SC&W profile      **b.** Election outcomes

**Fig. 2.7.** Comparing possible SC&W election outcomes

To the best of my knowledge, Brams' suggestion produced the first (and only) data set for a truly contested AV election. This profile can be used to compare how the outcomes of different procedures agree or differ; it can be used to determine whether the AV outcome matched standard claims made by its supporters. (It does not.) Brams and Peter Fishburn, the main proponents of Approval Voting, provided one analysis of the data (Brams and Fishburn [**14**]); I was asked to give another one (Saari [**59**]).

Who should have been the SC&W winner? While the Fig. 2.7a data designates $A$ as the plurality winner, the reader probably is becoming leery about trusting plurality outcomes. While $B$ is the antiplurality winner, this procedure is not much better. Therefore, it is worth examining what happens for other positional methods.

The procedure line for this data, depicted in Fig. 2.7b, proves that the only SC&W positional winners could be $A$ or $B$; candidate $C$ always is bottom ranked. In particular, $A$ wins with those methods which place light weight on a voter's second-ranked candidate while $B$ wins with the Borda Count and all procedures placing more weight on a voter's second-ranked candidate. (By finding the $s$ value with an $A \approx B$ tie, it follows that $B$ would win with all $\mathbf{w}_s = (1, s, 0)$ methods where $s > \frac{5}{11}$; i.e., $B$ would win with over half of the positional methods including the Borda Count.)

Providing added support for the sense that $B$ is the voters' true choice, the Fig. 2.7a tallies also show that $B$ is the Condorcet winner. Namely, $B$ beats both $A$ and $C$ in pairwise elections. Also, since $C$ loses to both $A$ and $B$ in pairwise votes, $C$ is the Condorcet loser.

**4.2. AV outcome for the SC&W election.** Let me be one of those "The Butler did it!" spoilsports by blurting out that, in conflict with a major claim made about Approval Voting, the Condorcet winner $B$ was *not* the SC&W winner. The AV outcome for this profile was $A \succ B \succ C$ with a 22:20:9 tally, so $A$ became the new SC&W president.

To understand what happened while identifying all possible AV outcomes for this profile, remember that AV allows each voter to vote for one, or for two, candidates. Consequently, as suggested by the earlier "teacher choice" story (page 23), expect the election outcome to vary depending on what the different voters choose to do. The goal is to use geometry to indicate how widely the AV outcomes can vary.

To see how to analyze this method, first consider the unanimity case where all voters have the $A \succ B \succ C$ preference. If all of them vote only for $A$, then the normalized election outcome is the point $(1, 0, 0)$. Remember, the first coordinate in this listing of election outcomes represents the electoral fortunes of $A$, so the "1" represents $A$'s unanimous victory. The other extreme has all voters voting for $A$ and $B$; the normalized outcome of

$(\frac{1}{2}, \frac{1}{2}, 0)$ means that $A$ and $B$ each receive half of the total vote, so it represents a $A \approx B$ tie with no votes for $C$. More generally, some voters vote only for $A$ while the rest vote for both $A$ and $B$. This $(x, 1 - x, 0)$ outcome lies between $(1, 0, 0)$ and $(\frac{1}{2}, \frac{1}{2}, 0)$ where the exact location is determined by the fraction $x$ of the voters who vote only for $A$.

The description for any specified profile is computed in a similar manner. First, find the smallest and largest number of points a candidate could receive in the Approval Voting election; e.g., the SC&W values follow.

(15)

| **High-low AV tallies** | $A$ | $B$ | $C$ |
|---|---|---|---|
| Lowest tally | 24 | 19 | 9 |
| Highest tally | 35 | 41 | 28 |

The exact number of votes a SC&W candidate receives is based on how many second-place votes he obtains; it is somewhere between these extremes. Since there are 12 different possible tallies for $A$, 23 for $B$, and 20 for $C$, *this one profile allows 5520 different Approval Voting election tallies.* As true with the teacher's choice story, these various outcomes capture all ways the different voters decide to mark their ballots.

To deliver on my promise to show a method with more varied election outcomes than anything ever permitted by the procedure line, notice how Table 15 allows *each SC&W candidate to be AV victorious;* even $C$ could win. In comparison, the procedure line allows only $A$ and $B$ to be elected, and a victory requires adopting different election procedures. AV, however, allows $A$, or $B$, or $C$ to be elected — not by changing the procedure or preferences, but with any change which influences whether voters vote for one or for two candidates. Scenarios supporting the election of each candidate are described later.

Nobody will willingly plot all 5520 normalized outcomes. So, to find a convenient geometrical representation of all possible AV election outcomes, start by computing and then plotting the $2^3 = 8$ normalized election points constructed by mixing and matching the extreme tallies for each candidate. Namely, plot the eight points representing the high and low tally for each candidate:

$$\tfrac{1}{52}(24, 19, 9), \quad \tfrac{1}{74}(24, 41, 9), \quad \tfrac{1}{71}(24, 19, 28), \quad \tfrac{1}{93}(24, 41, 28),$$
$$\tfrac{1}{63}(35, 19, 9), \quad \tfrac{1}{85}(35, 41, 9), \quad \tfrac{1}{82}(35, 19, 28), \quad \tfrac{1}{104}(35, 41, 28).$$

Next, find the convex hull defined by these eight points. (That is, connect each pair of vertices with straight lines. The resulting figure and its interior defines the hull.) Think of this as stretching a rubber sheet to attach it to the eight points. This sheet defines all possible AV outcomes. In other words, the importance of this hull, this "stretched rubber sheet" which is depicted by the shaded region in Fig. 2.7b, is that any of its points[8] could be the actual AV outcome for the specified profile.

**4.3. Possible election outcomes.** Because this expansive AV hull meets all 13 ranking regions, it follows that *not only could any of the three candidates have been victorious with AV, but any of the 13 ways to rank the candidates could have been the Approval Voting election outcome for this SC&W profile.* The source of the indecisiveness is clear; the actual election outcome is not based so much on the preferences of the voters as on outside conditions motivating who is, and is not, encouraged to vote for more than one candidate.

As an illustration of what could have happened:

1. Even though $C$ is bottom ranked with any standard election procedure, he could win the AV election by campaigning. Just by encouraging voters ranking $C$ in second place to vote for him, while $A$ and $B$ receive mainly top-place votes (which actually happened), $C$ would win.

2. Similarly, $B$ would win by persuading just three of $A$'s or $C$'s supporters to also vote for him. Notice how this "sensitivity" property, where a few voters can alter the conclusion, holds for any AV tally near a tied election. As Fig. 2.7b shows, AV admits many such situations.

3. A scenario which allows $A$ to win is what probably happened. With any highly competitive election, the natural strategic inclination is to vote for only one candidate. After all, voting for both main candidates risks "throwing away your vote." Indeed, even though all candidates were highly regarded, *only one voter represented in Fig. 2.7a voted for a second candidate.* This experience suggests that in competitive settings, where the choice of a procedure is important, the voters' natural strategic inclinations returns us to a de facto plurality vote — the precise procedure AV hopes to avoid.

**4.4. General AV properties.** The Fig. 2.7b embedding of the procedure line within the AV hull always must happen. To see why, notice that the plurality and antiplurality outcomes always are two of the eight plotted vertices. Consequently that "stretched rubber band" defining the procedure line is a strip within the stretched rubber sheet defining the AV hull.

An immediate consequence is that *for any profile, any undesired or troubling election outcome that results from the use of some positional method*

---

[8]More precisely, any of 5520 points within this hull could represent one of the 5520 different possible election outcomes for this profile. These points would be equally distributed within the hull if the tallies were not projected to the unit simplex.

*must be an admissible AV outcome. Moreover, AV allows many other elec-tion outcomes that never can occur with a positional method.*

To illustrate this last comment, notice that all positional tallies of the Fig. 2.8a profile share the same normalized outcome of $(\frac{6}{15}, \frac{5}{15}, \frac{4}{15})$; this is the bullet in Fig. 2.8b. With this surprising agreement, this lack of conflict, the procedure line collapses to a "procedure point" given by the bullet. The unanimity in normalized tallies and the pairwise outcomes for this profile, which all yield the same $A \succ B \succ C$ ranking, strongly suggest that this is the correct collective judgment of the voters.

The story radically changes with Approval Voting; this one profile allows 127,551 different normalized AV tallies. Again, these tallies are so widely varied that any of the thirteen ways to rank the three candidates is an admissible AV election outcome. This can be seen from the AV hull which is found by plotting the eight points which come from mixing-and-matching values from the following different tallies.

(16)

| High-low AV tallies | A | B | C |
|---|---|---|---|
| Lowest tally | 60 | 50 | 40 |
| Highest tally | 120 | 100 | 80 |

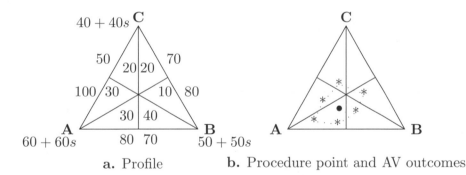

**a.** Profile     **b.** Procedure point and AV outcomes

**Fig. 2.10.** Another comparison

The approximate locations of these points (two are on the "procedure point") are the *'s in Fig. 2.8b. Connecting the *'s (with the dotted lines) to create the AV hull proves that instead of the $A \succ B \succ C$ common conclusion, the AV outcome could be the opposing $C \succ B \succ A$, or $C \succ A \approx B$, or any possible way to rank these three candidates. The actual outcome, then, resembles a gambler's lottery which depends on behavioral factors to influence how various individuals select to vote.

**4.5. Agree to strongly disagree.** Brams and Fishburn on one side, and I on the other, have agreed to strongly disagree about AV. To outline the differences, after it was discovered that a single profile can generate all sorts of AV outcomes (Saari and Van Newenhizen [**66**]), our differing views emphasize how the AV flexibility will be used (Brams, Fishburn, Merrill [**15**], Saari, Van Newenhizen [**67**]).

To explain, a fixed profile normally defines a fixed election outcome. Any disturbing properties of this outcome come from the procedure's mathematical structure. By understanding the mathematical source of the difficulties, problems can be corrected or a particular procedure avoided. In other words, this analysis emphasizes a mathematical, scientific study.

As shown with the 52-voter SC&W profile, Approval Voting allows a fixed profile to admit thousands of different outcomes. Included are all those outcomes which come from *any* positional method — no matter how troublesome the result may be — and then many, many more. If this were all that could be said about AV, the procedure would probably be dismissed as creating a societal lottery for the outcome. So, to seriously accept AV, someone needs to predict which of the radically different societal outcomes will be selected. As the answer cannot be further refined from the properties of the method, it must be based on the voters' *behavioral properties*, such as attitudes and emotions, on election day. In other words, a crucial step in analyzing AV falls within the realm of the behavioral sciences; any characterization or prediction that AV will produce a certain type of outcome requires accurately predicting how the voters always will behave.

Indeed, Brams and Fishburn (e.g., see their book [**13**]) introduce behavioral scenarios and assumptions where the AV outcome tends to elect the Condorcet winner. I'm a mathematician, so I cannot professionally evaluate whether their behavioral assumptions capture how voters always think. But I doubt it; beyond their arguments are thousands upon thousands of other possible and valid AV behavioral scenarios.

This describes our differences; I worry about those thousands of other possible AV outcomes, such as the actual SC&W election result, which do not fit their story. Namely, in a "real world" — or even in a broader based "theoretical world" — we should worry about what happens when voters are careless, or for strategic reasons they vote for only one candidate, or about what happens when there are high emotions caused by election rhetoric, perhaps a sense of revenge, maybe a wish to encourage minor candidates, or even the actions of small groups representing the so-called lunatic fringe. These events which manifest actual behavior involve actions that are far removed from the Brams and Fishburn positive description of voting behavior. For any important election outcome, all of these differences which could lead to unwelcomed societal outcomes become a realistic concern.

**4.6. President Perot?** By using my geometric approach, Tabarrok [**78**] proved that if AV had been used in the 1992 election, *anyone could have* *won;* AV would have made it possible to have President Perot. An electing scenario is where many of the voters who ranked Perot second vote for him — perhaps with the innocent intention of encouraging his views. But the closely contested election would make it unlikely for the voters ranking Clinton then Bush or Bush then Clinton to have voted for their second choice.

A more malicious scenario has Clinton voters, or Bush voters, trying to embarrass their main opponent. To do so, they also vote for Perot so the "minor candidate's" vote is near, or above, that received by the main opponent. This attitude could have elected Perot. In fact, with emotions and tensions rising near the end of the 2000 election, while highly unlikely, such an attempt to embarrass the opposition could have resulted in an AV election of President Nader.

The reader can explore other AV scenarios. To suggest where to look, recognize that in any election with a close outcome, the conclusion can be determined by a small number of voters. Positional procedures limit how such a division can occur. On the other hand, even in seemingly conclusive elections, as with the Fig. 2.10a profile, all AV tallies near a solid "tied outcome" line in Fig. 2.10b permit a small number of voters to change the outcome. Rather than being "high minded," their motivation may represent errors in marking ballots (as Florida proved, this happens!) or just being malcontents. It is worth worrying whether AV elections are lotteries where the spinning of the wheel comes from election emotions and hurt feelings.

**4.7. A political firestorm!** The structure developed to analyze AV extends to all procedures which allow more than one way to tally the ballots. This includes cumulative voting and the often suggested, "How about giving a voter 10 votes, and then ... " I will outline how to handle cumulative voting and leave the "divide 10 points" analysis to the reader.

In April, 1993, President Clinton nominated Lani Guinier to the Justice Department to handle civil rights issues. This nomination unleashed a firestorm of controversy. Some senators even labeled Guinier as a "dangerous radical" because of her advocacy of extreme voting procedures such as cumulative voting. Of course, silence from certain senators covered their embarrassment when they discovered that the conservative Reagan and Bush administrations also endorsed this approach.

What is this procedure and what are its properties? To consider a special case, suppose each voter has two points which can be assigned to one candidate, or split between two candidates. To analyze what can happen, do as above; compute the high and low scores for each candidate, plot the normalized outcomes, and then hook a rubber sheet on all of the points.

To illustrate what can happen, I will compute a couple of the points with the SC&W data of Fig. 2.7a; the rest of the computations are left to the interested reader. All points are determined by the eight extreme combinations based on whether the voters vote for one or two candidates. For instance, if all voters give both points only to their top-ranked candidate, then the $A \succ B \succ C$ tally is 48:38:18. If everyone votes for two, then the $B \succ A \succ C$ outcome is 41:35:28. Next, if only $C$ voters give both points to him, while all other voters vote for two candidates, the $C \succ A \succ B$ outcome has a 37:35:32 tally.

It is not necessary to continue; as with AV; once these points are plotted, any one of these three candidates could be elected depending on the "correct" scenario. In fact, the list of potential outcomes resembles the scatter on a shotgun target. With the wide array of shot in the target, there is a need to justify why we should expect one over the other. This is what Ms. Guinier does in her book [21] "The Tyranny of the Majority." But, Guinier offers limited strategies where minorities "bullet vote" to elect their candidates. What bothers me are the many other scenarios where voters in the majority could counter the actions of the minority by voting in blocs. Indeed, as we already have learned, a wide array of other, maybe unexpected, behavior is allowed by this analysis.

## 5. More candidates — toward Lincoln's election

I try to emphasize three-candidate settings primarily because it allows me to illustrate what happens while avoiding overly technical details. However, four candidates are needed to illustrate certain election difficulties. Also, I want to briefly discuss the Abraham Lincoln election which involved four candidates. As such, it is worth indicating how all of the geometric constructions extend to four or more candidates.

**5.1. Four candidates.** With four candidates, the triangle no longer suffices. To retain many of the tools of studying election outcomes, replace the triangle with a geometric object with four vertices which are an equal distance apart; this is the equilateral tetrahedron of Fig. 2.9a.

The idea is the same; identify each of the four candidates $\{A, B, C, D\}$ with a vertex of an equilateral tetrahedron as illustrated in Fig. 2.9a. Again, the ranking assigned to a point in the tetrahedron is determined by its distances to each vertex where "closer is better." This relationship divides the tetrahedron into 24 smaller tetrahedrons where each small region represents one of the $4! = 24$ ways to strictly rank the four candidates. Of course, for $N \geq 5$ alternatives, the appropriate object is an equilateral simplex which dwells only in an $(N - 1)$-dimensional space.

Even the three-dimensional tetrahedron is difficult to envision, so open it up. To do so, select a vertex, cut down the three connecting edges, and flatten the object to create the large equilateral triangle illustrated in Fig. 2.9b. For the Fig. 2.9 grand opening of the tetrahedron, I cut down the three edges connecting vertex $D$ with the three other vertices. In the flattened tetrahedron, the ranking associated with each of the 24 ranking regions still is determined by the distance to each vertex. In this way, the ranking associated with the small triangle with a "•" is $D \succ B \succ C \succ A$.

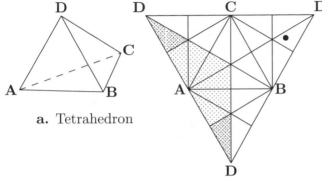

**a.** Tetrahedron

**b.** Flattened tetrahedron

**Fig. 2.9.** The representation tetrahedron

Again, represent a profile by placing the number of voters with a particular ranking in the appropriate ranking region. As before, the geometry facilitates the computation of election tallies. With four candidates, a normalized form of a positional method is $(1, s_1, s_2, 0)$ where $0 \le s_2 \le s_1 \le 1$. $A$'s plurality tally is computed by adding the numbers in the six ranking regions with $A$ as a vertex; these are the numbers that would be in the lightly shaded regions of Fig. 2.9b.

For the rest of the tally, $s_1$ is multiplied times the sum of numbers in the six ranking regions which have an edge on the lightly shaded region. Finally, $s_2$ is multiplied times the sum of numbers in the remaining six ranking regions where a vertex, but not an edge, is on the boundary of the lightly shaded region. These values are then added to the plurality tally.

It is interesting to know how to compute the outcome for a triplet. Actually, it is not difficult. If $D$ is not being considered, then the $D \succ A \succ B \succ C$ voters are one of the two types inherited by $A$ for her plurality tally for the triplet $\{A, B, C\}$. So, $A$'s tally becomes the sum of the numbers in the eight shaded regions. To find $A$'s $(1, s, 0)$ tally, add $s$ times the sum of the numbers in the eight regions with an edge or a vertex on one of the two long edges of the shaded region. Finally, $A$'s tally in a $\{A, B\}$ pairwise vote is the sum of the entries in the twelve regions to the left of the center dividing line; $A$'s tally in a $\{A, D\}$ pairwise vote is the sum of entries in the twelve regions in the square which includes the lightly shaded region and where one of its edges connects the $C$ and $B$ vertices.

This tallying procedure is illustrated in Fig. 2.10. For instance, $B$'s tally with four candidates is $7s_1$. Using the approach to find her outcome when considering only $\{A, B, C\}$, the 3 in the upper right-hand corner becomes a "first-place vote" and the two closest "2's" are second-place, so she receives $3 + 4s$ votes. I leave it as an amusing exercise for the reader to play with the geometry to discover how I designed this particular profile.

With the added flexibility granted by having more candidates, an exercise of the Fig. 2.9 type of creating paradoxical examples is easy to carry out. Start by placing numbers near the four vertices to create a specified plurality ranking. By moving these numbers in a manner to keep fixed plurality tallies, but in different positions relative to the other vertices, all sorts of surprising election examples can be discovered.

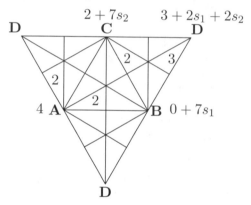

**Fig. 2.10.** The Eq. 9 profile and its positional tallies

### 5.2. Procedure line to triangle.
The opened tetrahedron provides a way to represent profiles and compute tallies. It remains to replace the procedure line with a different geometric representation of the election outcomes.

To keep from being overly abstract, concentrate on four candidates and use the tetrahedron from Fig. 2.9a to represent election tallies. Namely, a vertex of this tetrahedron represents an election tally where that candidate wins unanimously by garnering all possible points. How close a point inside the tetrahedron is to that vertex represents that candidate's normalized tally. The extreme is any point on the face opposite the vertex; it is where the candidate loses ignobly by not receiving even one point.

Extending the idea of a procedure line, all of a profile's positional outcomes can be represented with a "procedure triangle." To find this triangle for a profile, compute and plot the "vote for one" (plurality vote), "vote for two," and "vote for three" normalized election outcomes in the tetrahedron. Then, stretch a rubber sheet to attach it to the three plotted points. Any point on this rubber sheet — this procedure triangle — is the normalized election tally for some positional method.

For instance, the $(4, 7s_1, 2 + 7s_2, 3 + 2s_1 + 2s_2)$ tallies of the Eq. 9 (or Fig. 2.10) four-candidate profile have the normalized form of

$$\frac{1}{7(1 + s_1 + s_2)}(4, 7s_1, 2 + 7s_2, 3 + 2s_1 + 2s_2);$$

this normalized outcome is one of the points on the profile's procedure triangle. The precise location, which extends Eq. 14 from three alternatives to four, is determined by the expression

$$(17) \qquad \mathbf{q}^4_{(s_1,s_2)} = (1 - 2t_1 - t_2)\mathbf{q}^4_{(0,0)} + 2(t_1 - t_2)\mathbf{q}_{(1,0)} + 3t_2\mathbf{q}^4_{(1,1)}$$

where $t_1 = \frac{s_1}{1+s_1+s_2}$ and $t_2 = \frac{s_2}{1+s_1+s_2}$.

Using the above expression, mark with a dot the location of a particular procedure on the unstretched rubber sheet. When this "procedure triangle" is stretched to connect the three plotted points, the location of the dot identifies the normalized tally of that method.

**5.3. Could Lincoln have lost the 1860 election?** Leading up to the 1860 election, tensions within the United States were building to the point that even the existence of this country became questionable. Several states threaten to secede from the Union should Abraham Lincoln be successful. They did when Lincoln won the Presidency with with a majority vote in the Electoral College but a slim plurality vote.

The importance of this contentious election, among John Bell, John Breckinridge, Stephen Douglas, and Lincoln, attracted the attention of several scholars including William Riker [38]. To analyze this election, and to determine whether someone other than Lincoln could have been elected with a different procedure, Riker used historical sources to construct a probable profile of the voters at that time. In this manner, Riker computed the BC election ranking establishing that Douglas — not Lincoln — would have been the winner!

In an interesting paper published in 1999, Alex Tabarrok and Lee Spector described a new, more complete analysis of this important election [79]. They wanted to know "Was Lincoln's victory sound or was it due to a fluke in the electoral system? Did a Lincoln win plausibly represent the will of the voters or would a different voting system have represented their preferences more accurately?" Stated in another manner, they wanted to go beyond

Riker's limited conclusions to understand what could have happened with all possible positional methods. Their goal, by doing so, was to reach a more measured opinion as to the voters' true choice in the 1860 election.

To handle this problem, they used the above procedure triangle. This means that they needed to compute the normalized outcomes for the "vote for one," the "vote for two," and the "vote for three" election procedures. These computations require fairly complete information about the profile. Riker had one such data set.

Rather than relying just on Riker's data, Tabarrok and Spector surveyed one hundred historians who had written on the Civil War era. These experts were asked, based on their studies, to give their professional estimates on the division of the American voters during this 1860 election. Not all historians responded, and some had incomplete responses or felt unqualified. Out of the thirteen useful responses, Tabarrok and Spector computed what they called the "Mean Historian Profile."

Representing both profiles in the geometric manner of Fig. 2.11, it is interesting to see how they differ. (Incidentally, a data typo that is in [**79**] is corrected here.) The numbers are given in terms of percentages where, because of the usual rounding off errors, the sums do not always equal what they should. In this figure, L, D, B, and Br represent, respectively, Lincoln, Douglas, Bell, and Breckinridge.

As both data sets make clear, while Lincoln enjoyed a top ranking with about 39.8% of the voters, he had a polarizing effect on the American scene where a large number of voters ranked him at the bottom. (This is the sum of the numbers in the B-D-Br smaller triangle most distant from the L vertex.) No candidate, other than Breckinridge (the numbers in the center L-D-B triangle) suffered such a heavy negative reaction. In fact, the negatives for Lincoln's chief opponent, Stephen Douglas (the sum of the numbers in the L-B-Br triangle which is in the upper left corner) are negligible.

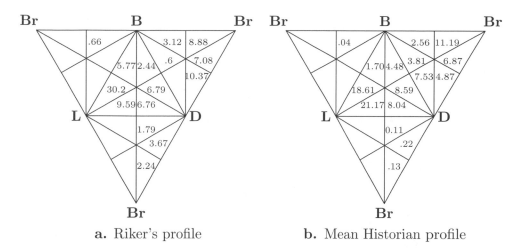

**a.** Riker's profile      **b.** Mean Historian profile

**Fig. 2.11.** Profiles for the 1860 election

While both figures show that Riker and the historians viewed Lincoln as distinctly less popular than Douglas, the data also proves that the historians had a dimmer view of Lincoln's popularity. For instance, by summing the numbers on each side of the vertical line separating "L" and "D" in each figure, it follows that Riker believes that Lincoln would have lost a "head-to-head" election with Douglas by receiving about 46% of the vote to Douglas's 54%, but the historians believe that Lincoln would have done more poorly by gaining only about 42% of the vote to Douglas's 58%. Both data sets show that Lincoln would have lost with an Instant Runoff Procedure.

(18)

|  | **Riker's profile** | **Historian's profile** |
|---|---|---|
| **Lincoln** | $39.79 + 14.32s_1 + 15.8s_2$ | $39.78 + 9.85s_1 + 13.46s_2$ |
| **Douglas** | $29.41 + 21.95s_1 + 47.97s_2$ | $29.36 + 36.46s_1 + 34.06s_2$ |
| **Bell** | $12.59 + 45.87s_1 + 33.8s_2$ | $12.59 + 45.92s_1 + 40.95s_2$ |
| **Breckinridge** | $18.2 + 17.82s_1 + 2.39s_2$ | $18.19 + 7.69s_1 + 11.45s_2$ |

**1860 Positional election tallies**

It is interesting to determine how the different candidates would have fared under different $\mathbf{w}_{s_1,s_2} = (1, s_1, s_2, 0)$, $1 \geq s_1 \geq s_2 \geq 0$, voting systems. The Table 18 tallies also demonstrate Lincoln's general unpopularity.

To analyze this data, Tabarrok and Spector plotted the procedure triangle in a tetrahedron. To do this, three normalized points need to be computed — the normalized outcome of the "vote for one" approach (the first data column in the following listing of Riker's data), the normalized "vote for two" outcome (half of each entry in the second data column), and the normalized 'vote for three" (one third of each entry in the third column). Think of these points as pulling on a rubber sheet; the convex hull identifies all possible positional outcomes.

|  | $(1,0,0,0)$ | $(1,1,0,0)$ | $(1,1,1,0)$ |
|---|---|---|---|
| **Lincoln** | 39.79 | 54.11 | 69.91 |
| **Douglas** | 29.41 | 51.36 | 99.30 |
| **Bell** | 12.59 | 58.46 | 92.26 |
| **Breckinridge** | 18.20 | 36.02 | 38.41 |

(19)

**Riker's Data**

Although the procedure triangle is not plotted here, the vertices already display some of the fascinating conclusions described in their paper [**79**]. For instance, as a student learning about this 1860 election, I had the impression that Breckinridge was the third strongest candidate while Bell was the weakest. The data shows that this is not the case; Breckinridge is the only candidate who could not have won with any positional procedures.

If the country had used a "vote for two" procedure, Riker's data suggests that we might be reading about President Bell. By plotting the procedure triangle, it becomes clear that Bell, or Douglas, or Lincoln could have been elected with an appropriate procedure. But most methods would have left us reading about President Douglas, and, perhaps, no mention of a non-existent Civil War. The fact that most voting approaches would not have favored Lincoln dramatically underscores the lessons learned in that history class; Lincoln was unpopular with many voters.

The historian's data, which follows, provides a very similar message; the main difference is that their data indicates that Douglas was even stronger favored than Riker assumed.

|  | $(1,0,0,0)$ | $(1,1,0,0)$ | $(1,1,1,0)$ |
|---|---|---|---|
| **Lincoln** | 39.78 | 49.63 | 63.09 |
| **Douglas** | 29.36 | 65.82 | 99.88 |
| **Bell** | 12.59 | 58.51 | 99.46 |
| **Breckinridge** | 18.19 | 25.88 | 37.33 |

(20)

**Historian's Data**

Steeped in the history of what did occur, and the leadership Lincoln exhibited during the Civil War, many readers probably join me in admiring President Lincoln and the role he played. Of course, it is impossible to compare what *did* happen with what *might have* happened. For instance, would "President Douglas" have avoided the strongly divisive Civil War, a war where repercussions, such as the design of "state flags," continue to remind us of the past? Nobody knows.

If Douglas could have steered the country through those troubled times without the cost of so many deaths, then we should bemoan the fact that a flawed election procedure elected the "wrong" person. On the other hand, maybe the times required the leadership of Lincoln. If so, then, while it is not appropriate to hope a distinctly unfavorable candidate will win because of a flawed election procedure — an event that often can and has caused serious societal damage — maybe we should be pleased that the "wrong" candidate won in 1860. But we never will know which would have been the better situation.

As a concluding comment, we might wonder what could have happened if Approval Voting had been used in this election. Again, the answer comes from plotting the hull of possible election outcomes. Again, to do so, take one of the two extreme outcomes for each candidate from Table 19, normalize this point, and plot it. This means that there are $2 \times 2 \times 2 \times 2 = 16$ points to plot. Then, connect these points. Any point in the resulting hull is an admissible election outcome. Because the procedure triangle always is inside the AV hull, it follows that far more election outcomes could result from AV than from any positional method; i.e., any ranking not having Breckinridge top ranked is a possible AV outcome.

**5.4. How bad can election outcomes get?** Let me conclude this chapter with some technical remarks and notes that are intended primarily for experts. To find everything that can happen in a multicandidate election (and this is the source of some of the earlier stated results), find all admissible locations of a procedure simplex. In turn, this requires finding all constraints which can be imposed on the vertices — the normalized tallies when the voters vote for a specified number of candidates.

To find lower bounds on these normalized tallies, when the voters vote for $k$ candidates, a candidate's tally must be at least what she would have received if they were asked to vote for $(k - 1)$ candidates. But when the voters vote for $(k - 1)$ and for $k$ candidates, the total tally is, respectively, $(k - 1)$ and $k$ times the number of voters. This means that

> for each $k \geq 2$, a candidate's normalized tally received when the voters vote for $k$ candidates is no less than $(k-1)/k$ times the candidate's normalized tally when the voters vote for $(k-1)$ candidates.

The upper bound is determined by the maximum number of votes a candidate could received. When voters vote for $k$ candidates, no candidate can receive more than $1/k$ of the total vote. Thus, each component of the normalized election tally for a "vote for $k$-candidate" procedure is no larger than $\frac{1}{k}$.

It turns out that these are the only constraints on the normalized election tallies. This means that any manner a simplex can be positioned where the vertices have these conditions (and all components are rational) corresponds to the set of positional election tallies for some profile.

So how varied and bad can the election outcomes be? Quite bad. This is because any of the geometric ways a simplex can be positioned to cross ranking regions defines another list of unexpected, paradoxical outcomes. This means examples can be created to be as wild and counter-intuitive as desired.

A partial listing of what can happen is captured by Thm. 3 which shows how rapidly it can be that a profile allows millions to billions to trillions of different positional election rankings. This result follows by geometrically determining the limits on the number of regions such a simplex can cross.

I also asserted in Thm. 4 that once there are four or more alternatives, it is possible to have a profile where different positional methods rank each candidate in first, second, third, ... , last place. This conclusion is a direct consequence of determining the variety of ranking regions a simplex can meet. For three candidates, however, the procedure simplex is a line, so the geometry imposes strong restrictions on what regions it can cross.

While the analysis for the statistical and power indices assertions differ from the above in technical details, these assertions still retain much of the geometric spirit. The differing possible outcomes can be captured on a simplex which has much of the above properties.

# Chapter 3

# Chaotic Election Outcomes

A surprising level of uncomfortable electoral ambiguity arises by using different methods to tally the same ballots. Indeed, the same candidate with the same data could be ranked first with one method, but last with another. All of this variation should cause pause and reflection about what that last election outcome which was important for you, whatever it involved, actually meant.

To avoid these electoral problems, all sorts of election techniques have been invented. I already mentioned the Instantaneous Runoff Method. As another example, a mathematics department in the midwest uses a complicated "runoff" method. This selection process — for hiring purposes, to select a new calculus book, etc. — involves several plurality elections. At each step, they drop the bottom-ranked alternatives and then have another election.

Indeed, it may have been when I was the chair of the mathematics department at Northwestern University when we refined our election procedure for the all important Budget Committee. With the new method, at the first stage, everyone voted for four candidates. The top six candidates from the first election are advanced to runoff; everyone again voted for four candidates and the ranking of the runoff determined the four committee members. (Later I will describe how and why this procedure was modified.)

Are these reasonable methods? Without question, they provide a significant improvement over the straight plurality vote. But they have flaws;

there are better approaches. The arguments developed in this chapter provide the tools to make it easier to identify the possible failings.

Another issue, which is the basic theme of this chapter, is to understand what can happen when candidates withdraw. Will the choice of the election procedure make a difference in what can occur? These are the kinds of conclusions discussed here.

The chapter title is designed to warn the reader to expect the unexpected; expect chaotic appearing election outcomes. In fact, the connection is more intimate; as indicated at the end of the chapter, some of the results described in this chapter were first discovered by modifying notions coming from chaotic dynamics. Moreover, the methodology shows that these results are not restricted to voting; in Chapter 6 it is indicated how they extend to other aggregation procedures such as probability and statistics.

## 1. Deanna had to withdraw

One of the more important functions of any academic department is to make superb new hires. It is crucial for the department's future that excellence is identified and, if possible, hired. In precisely this spirit, after much debate, a mathematics department finally decided that the four finalists for their one tenure-track position are {Alice, Beth, Claire, Deanna}. The voters' preferences (see Fig. 3.1b.) are:

(21)

| Number | Ranking | Number | Ranking |
|--------|---------|--------|---------|
| 3 | $A \succ C \succ D \succ B$ | 2 | $C \succ B \succ D \succ A$ |
| 6 | $A \succ D \succ C \succ B$ | 5 | $C \succ D \succ B \succ A$ |
| 3 | $B \succ C \succ D \succ A$ | 2 | $D \succ B \succ C \succ A$ |
| 5 | $B \succ D \succ C \succ A$ | 4 | $D \succ C \succ B \succ A$ |

Here, the plurality election outcome is

$$\text{Alice} \succ \text{Beth} \succ \text{Claire} \succ \text{Deanna}.$$

The standard problem occurred. Right after the departmental election, but before anything could be done, Deanna called the Chair to withdraw her name; she just accepted a much better position elsewhere.

By Deanna withdrawing, the actual set of candidates becomes {Alice, Beth, Claire}. What should the department do? Should they hold another election? I know of no department that would even consider this. Instead, they would drop Deanna's name from the ranking and then offer the position to Alice.

This story describes what usually is done in practice. However, if the department did hold another election in this situation, they would discover that the new outcome becomes the *reversed*

$$\text{Claire} \succ \text{Beth} \succ \text{Alice.}$$

(The voters with Deanna as their first choice now vote for someone else.) In other words, maybe Claire, rather than Alice, should be offered the position.

The situation is much worse. Check; if any candidate or if any two candidates were to withdraw, then the election outcome would reverse from the original to be consistent with

$$\text{Deanna} \succ \text{Claire} \succ \text{Beth} \succ \text{Alice.}$$

For instance, if Alice and Claire were to withdraw, the outcome would have Deanna $\succ$ Beth; if Claire were to withdraw, the new outcome would be Deanna $\succ$ Beth $\succ$ Alice. With all of this added information, let me ask again, is top-ranked Alice, or is bottom-ranked Deanna, the true preferred choice of the department?

We might suspect that this changeable outcome illustrates still another failing of the plurality vote. It does, but the conclusion is more general. To see what else can occur, suppose an eleven-member College committee is charged with selecting the winner of a prestigious research prize. The committees profile for the candidates {Helina, Ingrid, Janice} is in Fig. 3.1a.

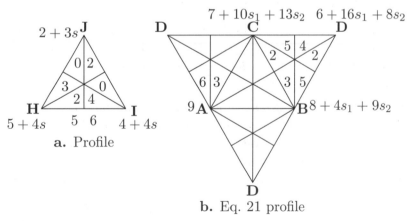

**a.** Profile

**b.** Eq. 21 profile

**Fig. 3.1.** Some profiles

The members of this committee were well aware of the potential dangers associated with election procedures. Therefore, they were delighted to discover that, whatever positional method they happened to use,

Helina always is the winner, Ingrid always is second ranked, and Janice always is in last place.

(As indicated in Fig. 3.1a, the $\mathbf{w}_s$ tallies are $(5+4s, 4+4s, 3+3s)$.) Comforted by this strong procedural agreement, the committee decided with confidence to use this common ranking to determine their decison; Helina would win the prize.

The night before the College meeting called to make the announcement, Janice learned about the committee ranking. To avoid being embarrassed by by coming in last, Janice asked to have her name withdrawn. The committee found this to be no problem. However, just as the Dean was calling on the committee chair to make the formal announcement, the chair glanced at the data and noticed that with Helina and Ingrid being the only two candidates,

this committee really preferred Ingrid over Helina.

What should this chair do? Who should win the prize?


## 2. General results

These two stories, which capture only a portion of what can happen, are generalized in the next statement.

**Theorem 6** (Saari [**40**]). *Suppose there are three or more candidates.*

- *Rank the candidates in any desired transitive manner. Next, select the positional election method to tally ballots.*

- *Drop one of the candidates. Rank the remaining candidates in any transitive manner. This ranking need not have anything to do with the original ranking. Next, select the positional election method to tally ballots.*

- *Continue this process of dropping a candidate, and then assigning a ranking and a positional procedure to the new set of candidates. The ranking at each stage need not be related, in any manner, with an earlier ranking. Continue until only a pair of candidates remains. Rank this pair and specify the majority vote as the election procedure.*

*There exists a profile so that when the voters vote on any of the above sets of candidates where ballots are tallied in the indicated manner, the election outcome is the specified one.*

This assertion is very discouraging. As a special case, it captures the worse nightmare that can be associated with a runoff or elimination procedure. Namely, this result establishes that there need not be any relationship whatsoever between the societal outcome for a set of all candidates and some subset of candidates.

For instance, this theorem means that it is possible to create a profile where its plurality ranking is

$$A \succ B \succ C \succ D \succ E \succ F,$$

but if $D$ drops out, the profile's BC ranking becomes the reversed

$$F \succ E \succ C \succ B \succ A,$$

when $E$ drops out its antiplurality ranking is the mixed

$$A \succ F \succ B \succ C,$$

when $F$ drops out its $(3, 1, 0)$ ranking is

$$B \succ C \succ A$$

even though $A$ beats $B$ in a two-person majority vote.

As such, the conclusion means for a runoff that after a bottom-ranked candidate is dropped, the new ranking can be the exact opposite. And then when the new bottom-ranked candidate is dropped, the ranking reverses again! (By the end of this section, the reader should be able to construct any number of illustrating examples.) While the plurality vote is particularly susceptible to this difficulty, the theorem asserts that this problem plagues all possible positional methods.

**2.1. Sydney, not Beijing, hosted the 2000 Olympics.** An actual situation where election outcomes could change as candidates are dropped comes from the selection of a site for the 2000 Olympic games. To set the stage, in 1993 there was a wide sense that Beijing was favored to be selected. After all, China has about 20% of the world's population, and it had been making huge strides toward improving living standards. While American politicians on both the Republican and Democrat sides opposed China's bid because of "human right violations," China did put forth a strong proposal along with promises to admit athletes from around the world. Sooner or later, the games will be in China, so, the feeling seemed to be, why not now? China was widely favored to win.

The procedure used in the selection process is a plurality runoff where the bottom-ranked city is dropped at each stage. At the end of the first round, Beijing was in first place. The election tallies were

> Beijing — 32 votes, Sydney — 30 votes, Manchester — 11 votes, Berlin — 9 votes, Istanbul — 7 voters.

By being bottom ranked, Istanbul was eliminated.

At the end of the second round, Beijing gained strength in its first-place hold over Manchester. The situation could only raise the spirits and expectations for China and her supporters. Indeed, the tallies of

Beijing — 37 votes, Sydney — 30 votes, Manchester — 13 votes, Berlin — 9 votes

showed that five of the previous Istanbul votes went to Beijing while Manchester got the other two. As Berlin did not receive any new support, the city was eliminated by being bottom ranked.

Although the situation looked encouraging for Beijing, the race grew tighter at the end of the third round. Here, the tallies

Beijing — 40 votes, Sydney — 37 votes, Manchester — 11 votes,

indicated a peculiarity; Manchester *lost two votes* and was eliminated.

Notice the pattern; each time a candidate was dropped, the new ranking religiously followed the original

Beijing $\succ$ Sydney $\succ$ Manchester $\succ$ Berlin $\succ$ Istanbul

ranking. This pattern, with the consistent dominance of Beijing through all the rounds of voting, created the widely held expectation that Beijing would win. The final round between Beijing and Sydney, however, caused joy "down-under" with extreme disappointment in China; Sydney won by 45-43. The outcome was so unexpected that the "choice of Sydney brought a gasp of surprise from the huge crowd ... The Australian delegation then jumped to its feet, yelling in glee, while the stunned Chinese delegation applauded politely."[1] Thereafter came various explanations and recriminations. Although political considerations most surely played a role in shaping the final decision, just by understanding how election rankings can change when candidates are dropped, as described next, this conclusion should not be overly surprising.

**2.2. Creating examples.** Before offering even more involved results about what can happen in elections, let me develop some intuition about why this conclusion holds — at least for the simpler setting of the plurality vote. To do so, I use the Fig. 3.2a profile which has the plurality ranking of

$A \succ B \succ C \succ D$ with a $21 : 20 : 19 : 18$ tally.

But, should $D$ drop out, the new plurality ranking becomes the reversed

$C \succ B \succ A$;

this result is true even though there appears to be a conflict because a majority of these voters prefer $A \succ C$.

---

[1]N.Y. Times, 9/23/93.

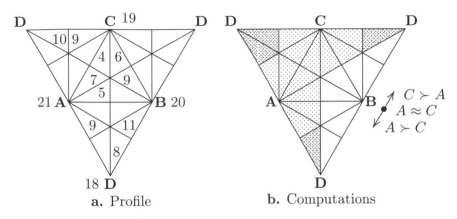

**Fig. 3.2.** Creating paradoxical outcomes

I purposely designed my explanation of this phenomenon, which uses the geometry of Fig. 3.2b, in a manner to show the reader how to create a variety of other surprising election examples. To start, notice that the line connecting vertices $D$ and $B$, which represents the $A \approx C$ region of indifference, splits the flattened tetrahedron into two equal parts. As the arrows on the right side of the tetrahedron indicate, the part of the tetrahedron which lies above this line has all of the preferences where the voters prefer $C$ to $A$; the portion below this line has all of the preferences where the voters prefer $A$ to $C$.

In the four-candidate election, $A$'s and $C$'s plurality votes are determined by the numbers which would be placed in the six lightly shaded regions on their respective sides of the $A \approx C$ line of the tetrahedron. These are the regions where the respective candidate is top ranked. With the Fig. 3.2a data, this gives $A$ and $C$, respectively, $7 + 5 + 9 = 21$ and $9 + 4 + 6 = 19$ votes.

When $D$ drops out, her votes are redistributed among the remaining three candidates. In particular, $A$ and $C$ each gain for their tallies the sum of values which would be listed in the two heavily shaded regions on their side of the $A \approx C$ line. To be more precise, notice that the heavily shaded region in the upper left corner below the $A \approx C$ line corresponds to the $D \succ A \succ C \succ B$ ranking. If $D$ resigns from the race, this ranking becomes $A \succ C \succ B$, so $A$ inherits all of these plurality votes.

So, for $C$ to be able to beat $A$, just design the example so that there are an appropriate number of extra votes in $C$'s two more heavily shaded regions. The effect of this added vote is illustrated with the Fig. 3.2a profile where $C$ picks up $10 + 0 = 10$ votes while $A$ picks up no extra support.

Finally the $\{A, C\}$ pairwise vote adds all of the values that are in the twelve regions on each side of the $A \approx C$ line. With respect to their three- and four-candidate elections, these regions give both $A$ and $C$ the added votes which come from the numbers in four extra regions. As such, it is easy to adjust values in these regions in a manner to permit $A$'s victory over $C$. (In the Fig. 3.2a profile, $A$ picks up $11 + 8 = 19$ more votes to $C$'s 9.) In other words, this geometric display of the extra information used by the different plurality tallies converts Thm. 6, when restricted to the plurality vote, from a surprise to a natural conclusion. With this intuition, the only unexpected assertion is that the statement holds for *all positional methods.*

With this description, the reader now should be able to construct several new examples exhibiting the hidden fears of the chair of any group. To be sure that the reader has captured the ideas, let me suggest the challenge of constructing a profile where the $A \succ B \approx C \succ D$ plurality outcome has the tallies 7:6:6:5. But, after dropping the bottom ranked $D$, the new plurality ranking reverses to $C \succ B \succ A$. Then, after dropping $A$, who was top ranked among all candidates but became bottom ranked in the three-candidate election, the outcome reverses to have $B$ beat $C$ in a pairwise majority vote. In fact, with only slightly more effort, the reader should be able to construct the profile so that it has the cyclic pairwise outcomes of $B \succ C$, then $C \succ A$, and finally $A \succ B$.

**2.3. The Lincoln-Douglas 1860 election.** To further illustrate the use of this geometry, let me describe what would have happened in the 1860 election if either Bell or Breckinridge had dropped out of the race before election day. According to Riker's data in Fig. 2.11 (page 65), Breckinridge dropping out of the campaign would have had absolutely no effect on Lincoln's vote; his tally would remain at 39.89% as the two small triangles are empty. Douglas, however, would have picked up $2.24\% + 7.08\% = 9.31\%$ of the total vote giving him the new tally of 38.72% of the popular vote. In other words, Lincoln still would have won the popular plurality vote, but the outcome would have allowed Douglas to come close to being in a plurality tie with Lincoln.

The historians' data, gathered by Tabarrok and Spector, offer a similar story. Again, their data show that Lincoln would not pick up any of the Breckinridge votes, but Douglas would pick up 6.90%.

Bell is the candidate with the smallest plurality vote. If he had dropped out, then, according to Riker's data, Lincoln would have picked up $5.77\% + 0\% = 5.77\%$ of the vote to Douglas's small $3.12\% + 0.6\% = 3.18\%$. This means that Lincoln would have enjoyed an even stronger plurality victory. The data from the historians slightly disagrees; while the data would have Lincoln picking up an additional $1.70\% + 0\% = 1.70\%$ of the total vote,

Lincoln still would win — but Douglas would have pulled closer — as the addition to Douglas's total is $3.81\% + 4.48\% = 8.29\%$.

So, had either of the two minor candidates dropped out, we still would have had President Lincoln. But, as earlier described, if both had dropped out, we would be discussing President Douglas. In other words, the pattern of the 1860 election follows that of the selection of the site for the 2000 Olympics; when bottom-ranked candidates are dropped, the nature of the ranking changes only at the last step.

**2.4. More extreme conclusions.** A lesson one quickly learns after studying voting procedures is that most of us incorrectly interpret what election outcomes mean. Consider, for instance, the problems facing the personnel search committee of a department. If our first choice is not available to hire, we do the obvious; we make an offer to the second-ranked choice without bothering to hold a new election. In other words, should a candidate drop out, fine, we tend to make the tacit, but probably incorrect assumption that a natural adjustment to the earlier election ranking accurately reflects our views. Theorem 6 indicates that these implicit assumptions can be false.

While Thm. 6 should cause concern, the actual situation can be much, much worse. Rather than limiting the results to settings where the election rankings can vary just within a restricted selection of subsets (nested) of candidates which are defined by successively dropping candidates, we must wonder whether election outcomes can have little or no relationship across all possible sets of candidates. After all, the earlier Eq. 21 and Fig. 3.1b profile demonstrated that not only could the election outcomes for the subsets of candidates differ, but they could be the complete reversal of the original ranking.

As asserted next, it is possible for the most wildly imaginable arrangement of election rankings to occur — not for all election procedures, but for almost all of them.

**Theorem 7** (Saari [**41, 57**]). *Let $N$ represent the number of candidates, and suppose there are at least three candidates.*

- *Rank the candidates in any desired transitive manner. Next, select the positional election method to tally ballots.*

- *There are $N$ ways to drop one of the candidates. For each of these ways, rank the remaining $(N-1)$ candidates in any desired transitive manner. These rankings need not have anything to do with one another or with the original ranking. Next, for each subset of candidates, select the positional election method to tally ballots.*

- *Continue this process. Namely, for each possible subset of three or more candidates, assign a transitive ranking and a positional voting procedure. The ranking need not be related, in any manner, to any of the other rankings.*

- *For each pair, assign a ranking; the voting procedure is the majority vote.*

*For almost all choices of positional voting methods,[2] and this includes the commonly used plurality vote, and the "vote for two," or "vote for three," or ... methods, there exists a profile so that when the voters vote on any of the above sets of candidates where ballots are tallied in the indicated manner, the election outcome is the specified one.*

*A voting method which does not allow this highly chaotic state of affairs is the Borda Count.*

This result already is partially demonstrated by the Eq. 21 and Fig. 3.1b profile where the plurality ranking of *each subset of candidates* — all triplets and all pairs — is the reverse of the four-candidate plurality ranking. The above assertion, however, proves that we should anticipate much wilder behavior.

Indeed, the outcomes can be much worse. For instance, the Fig. 3.2a profile exhibits a more extreme "flip-flop" behavior. Namely,

- the four-candidate plurality outcome is $A \succ B \succ C \succ D$,

- all three-candidate plurality elections agree with the opposite; they agree with $D \succ C \succ B \succ A$, and

- all pairwise majority votes flip again to agree with the original $A \succ B \succ C \succ D$ ranking.

Later in this chapter, I will briefly explore some of the consequences of this Thm. 7 assertion. For now, consider the common method of dropping bottom-ranked candidates. We all do this. After all, when large numbers of candidates — say, for the one position in a department — are being considered, the discussion often starts by trying to find reasons to *eliminate* candidates. This is why when helping graduate students prepare for a "job talk," or when we write a grant proposal, a first stage is to avoid providing "excuses" to be eliminated. On a more formal level, this dropping of a candidate defines the essence of methods such as the Instant Runoff Procedure, the voting approach I mentioned that is used by a midwestern mathematics

---

[2]More precisely, juxtapositioning the voting vectors assigned to each subset of candidates creates a vector in a Euclidean space with an appropriate dimension. In this space, there is a proper, lower-dimensional, algebraic variety $\alpha^N$. If the vector of juxtapositioned voting vectors belongs to this algebraic set, and the vector defined by always using the Borda Count is such an example, then not all ranking paradoxes can occur. This theorem applies to the complement of $\alpha^N$; thus most collections of voting vectors, which includes the common methods of always using the plurality vote, or the "vote for two" method, or ... , or of using any combination of these approaches, allow anything to occur.

department, the selection of the Budget Committee at Northwestern University, or even the selection of a site for the Olympics.

Theorem 7 can be used to show that while this dropping of a candidate is a very common practice, rather than ensuring a level of excellence, it can encourage mediocrity — or worse. After all, according to the theorem, profiles for 20 candidates can be constructed so that, with one exception, whenever $A$ is one of the candidates of a subset, she will be the plurality winner. This means she beats all candidates in head-to-head elections to become the Condorcet winner. This means that when compared with any two other candidates, or with any three other candidates, or ... she always wins. However, in the full set of 20 candidates, she has so many "second place votes" that she is plurality bottom ranked. As such, she is dropped with any runoff method. For me the data strongly suggests that $A$ is the group's true top choices even though she is the first to be dropped with a runoff.

It probably is a useful exercise for the reader to consider her or his favored election method. Then, with the help of Thm. 7, the reader should be able to construct examples illustrating what can go wrong. The answers can be discouraging. However, rest assured; starting in Chapter 5, I offer some positive comments.

## 3. Consequences

While Thm. 7 suggests that all sorts of unexpected and troubling election problems can arise, it also provides at least a glimmer of hope for consistency. The theorem has an escape clause suggesting that there is a way to avoid some of the horrific election paradoxes.

To review, the negative assertion and implications of Thm. 7 are constructed by using the flexibility allowed in election rankings. The potential positive sense comes from the loophole in the theorem which claims that "almost all" procedures allow any imaginable collection of rankings to occur. This exception suggests that maybe we should try to identify those rare, singular methods that will allow some consistency in election rankings. After all, if we can identify and then use those methods which are more trouble free, then we can ignore all those bothersome difficulties catalogued by Thm. 7 because they describe what happens with the rejected approaches.

First, some of the negative consequences of Thm. 7 are examined. Then, I will describe those voting methods which offer more consistency in election behavior.

**3.1. Creating problems.** I want to show how to use Thm. 7 to expose new problems with various methods that have been mentioned in earlier sections.

3.1.1. *Instant Runoff Procedure.* Earlier (page 19) I asserted that the Instant Runoff Procedure has flaws. Armed with Thm. 7 it is not hard to expose many of them. As just one example, suppose the four candidates $\{A, B, C, D\}$ are running to be the new mayor. According to the theorem, there are examples of profiles so that the plurality election ranking of all four candidates is

$$A \succ B \succ C \succ D,$$

even though, with one exception, the election rankings of all remaining subsets are consistent with the ranking

$$D \succ C \succ B \succ A; \text{ the exception is the pair where } A \succ B.$$

In other words, $D$ beats all candidates in pairwise elections and in all triplets. While $C$ consistently loses to $D$, with the exception of the first election, she always beats both $A$ and $B$.

Because of the myopic nature of this runoff method, the arguably favored candidates $D$ and $C$ are dropped at the first stage—they have too many supporters who have them second ranked. This advances $A$ and $B$ to the runoff where $A$ wins. This data sure appears to support the superiority of $D$ followed by $C$. However, nobody will ever know that they rejected the excellence of $D$ and $C$ because they are dropped at the end of the first round of the Instant Runoff Procedure. But $A$, who must be viewed as a somewhat inferior candidate as she would win in only two of the many possible elections, is the overall winner.

Here is another bothersome example. Suppose if the election were to be held today, Ann would be the Instant Runoff Winner. Pushing for victory, Ann's election eve appearance persuaded supporters of her main opponent, Beth, to now vote for her. But, by gaining support from the voters, Ann loses with the Instant Runoff procedure!

To see how this can happen, Thm. 7 ensures that a $A \succ B \approx C \succ D$ outcome can be accompanied by the pairwise rankings of $A \succ B$ and $C \succ A$. By continuity, this allows $A \succ B \succ C \succ D$ election outcomes where $Beth$ is barely ahead of $C$onnie, and where the pairwise outcomes remain $A \succ B$ and $C \succ A$. Because of Ann's persuasive appearance, $Beth$ *loses votes* at the first stage, so $A$nn and $C$onnie are advanced to the runoff. Here, $C$onnie, not $A$nn, is the winner. By the way, illustrating examples are not difficult to construct; a slight modification of the one suggested on page 76 suffices.

3.1.2. *More general runoffs.* As a further illustration, consider, for example, the method where after a plurality vote, the bottom one, or two, or three ranked candidates are dropped. Then another election is held. What can go wrong with this? To illustrate with four candidates (where the reader now should be able to construct illustrating examples), suppose that the bottom-ranked candidate is dropped. But, as already illustrated with the Eq. 21 profile, this could be a serious error. After all, the $A \succ B \succ C \succ D$ ranking, where $D$ will be dropped, could be in error because all other subsets of candidates would rank $D$ at the top.

How about ranking the candidates in a pairwise manner? Maybe the election can be something which resembles a tournament where only one candidate will emerge successful. After all, anything that is good for the National Basketball Association, or for the NCAA, should be good for the rest of society.

Nice idea, but it can have troubles. According to Thm. 7, it is entirely possible for the pairwise rankings to be consistent with $E \succ D \succ C \succ B \succ A$; this ranking indicates that candidate $E$ should be the societal choice. Adding doubt to this conclusion, however, is that the election ranking of *all other subsets of candidates* — when triplets are considered, or when sets of four, or when the full set are ranked with an election — the outcome is the precise opposite by being consistent with $A \succ B \succ C \succ D \succ E$. This uncomfortable fact is not restricted to the plurality vote; for almost all choices of voting methods, such an example can be created.

Do you want to show that with the same profile it is possible for different methods to elect different candidates? How about generating an example where each candidate wins with a different kind of elaborate voting approach. No problem.

To illustrate how to prove that such variety in winners can occur, with eight candidates, create a tournament with the appropriate seeding and where the winner of one competition is paired with the winner of another specified competition. Specify that $A$ is to win. (This uses up the rankings of seven pairs.)

Next, specify that $B$ is to win with an agenda; this is a form of a tournament where each winning candidate meets the next specified alternative. (This uses up the rankings of seven more pairs; so far, 14 of the 28 pairs are used.)

Next, require $C$ to be the winner of a procedure where, after the first election, all but the top three are eliminated; these three are reranked with another election.

I could go on and on, but the point is made; choose rankings for any of these procedures so that the specified candidate wins. As long as the different procedures are selected so that they do not require some set of candidates to have different rankings, Thm. 7 ensures that a profile can be created where the specified candidate wins with the specified procedure. What a mess!

**3.2. Avoiding problems.** Theorem 7 identifies the Borda Count as the only positional voting procedure which avoids many of the election ranking difficulties. The following describes some of its advantages.

1. One of the many above illustrations envisions a situation where the pairwise rankings are the exact opposite of the positional ranking of all pairs. In other words, consider the paradoxical setting where the majority vote ranking of any pair is consistent with $A \succ B \succ C \succ D \succ E \succ F$, but the positional ranking is the precise opposite $F \succ E \succ D \succ C \succ B \succ A$. This uncomfortable situation can occur with all positional methods except one — the Borda Count. For reasons explained later, the BC never allows a Condorcet winner to be bottom ranked; the BC always ranks the Condorcet winner above the Condorcet loser. No other positional procedure can guarantee these relationships. If fact, if the pairwise rankings are transitive, then the Borda winner always is ranked above the Borda loser. On the other hand, the plurality winner could be pairwise ranked below the plurality loser, and this is true for all other non-BC methods.

2. In fact, the BC is the *only* positional method where the way the pairs are ranked must be related to the BC ranking. This means, for instance, that with the exception of the BC, for any other positional method an example can be created where the pairwise ranking is consistent with

$$A \succ B \succ C \succ D \succ E \succ F$$

even though the positional method has the opposite

$$F \succ E \succ D \succ C \succ B \succ A,$$

or any other specified ranking. The reasons for this bothersome behavior are indicated in Chapter 5.

3. Suppose $A$ is the winner in all three-candidate subsets in which she is included. Can she be bottom ranked in the set of all candidates? With almost all positional procedures, this perverse outcome can occur. Only the BC and a highly restricted set of other procedures deny this paradoxical behavior.

4. This same behavior holds for subsets of candidates of any size. So, for all subsets of four, or five, or six candidates, a consistent Borda Count winner can never be BC bottom ranked in the set of all candidates, but such natural consistency conditions need not hold for other positional methods.

5. Other combinations of positional methods can create election relationships. However, some of the resulting relationships are perverse rather than helpful. For instance, it is possible to create natural methods (Saari [45]) where a candidate who consistently wins with one kind of procedure when used with certain subsets can win with all candidates only if she also is the *Condorcet loser!* (That is, if she loses all pairwise elections.) Such negative conclusions never can be associated with the Borda Count.

6. In fact, suppose someone discovers a listing of BC election rankings over the different subsets of candidates that appears to be troublesome. It turns out (Saari [41]) that *all other choices of positional procedures allows the precise same choice of rankings.* Indeed, an example can be constructed (Saari [57]) where all of the specified rankings arise with all procedures. On the other hand, any other collection of positional methods allows inconsistent election rankings that never could occur with the BC.

At the beginning of this chapter, when the voting approach for the Budget Committee of the mathematics department of Northwestern University was described, I mentioned that the method was subsequently modified. The new approach takes advantage of the virtues of the BC; the committee still is elected with the described runoff procedure, but the both elections are conducted with a form of the Borda Count.

Let me offer a "counting" measure which captures a sense of the improvements allowed by the Borda Count; to keep the numbers within reason, consider only six candidates. Start by listing for all subsets of candidates a ranking that can occur with the plurality vote; call it a "plurality word." For instance, one word is $A \succ B, A \succ C, B \succ C, B \succ A \approx C, \ldots$. Call the set of all distinct words that can be constructed the *plurality dictionary* of voting paradoxes. Now, do the same for the Borda Count to define the *BC dictionary* of voting paradoxes. The paradoxical outcomes, of course, are the words — listings of election rankings — which are unexpected and counterintuitive.

A way to compare two methods to determine how bad the situation can be is to compare the number of words that are in each dictionary. For instance, if the plurality dictionary has one hundred more words than the BC dictionary, that provides a sense about the number of added kinds of difficulties caused by the plurality vote. If the plurality dictionary has twice as many words, that indicates an even more troubling situation. What would you speculate as the difference?

The result is astronomical! Since even tie elections are allowed, there are more than $10^{50}$ more words — more lists of things that can go wrong — in the plurality dictionary than in the BC dictionary. This means that suppose someone discovers a list of rankings indicating what can go wrong with the Borda Count. There are more than $10^{50}$ ways to modify this list to indicate bothering plurality outcomes. To give a sense of what this means, suppose at the time of the big bang, a thousand of the world's fastest computers divided the work load and started counting; today, the set of these computers would be nowhere near listing these changes from just *one BC* list of rankings. It would take more than another thousand millennia to get there.

## 4. Chaotic notions for chaotic results

How were these voting results initially discovered? As stated in the preface, the main problem was to find a way to discover all possible "paradoxes"; that is, the goal was to find all behaviors that we do not expect to occur. How can this be done?

Actually, from the 1960s on, such a mathematical program of "finding and even cataloguing the unexpected" had been widely used in the area dynamical systems. To illustrate what happens, let me reach back to my high school days when I would occasionally hang out at the local pool hall.

**4.1. Lessons from a pool hall.** Anyone who has picked up a cue stick for the first time knows that after striking the cue ball, almost anything — or maybe nothing — can occur. With "this ball hitting that ball hitting some other ball," the resulting dynamic of balls flying in all directions on the table is a truly chaotic experience.

On the other hand, an expert wielding the cue stick with surgical precision can extract from this myriad of possible events a particularly desired one — say, "the one-ball hits the two-ball hits the three-ball hits the four-ball hits the five-ball hits the six-ball which goes into the far pocket." How is this done? As I will describe, it involves a filtering process; it involves an iterative refinement of the target area on the cue ball where it should be struck.

The first goal is to find where to strike the cue ball so that it will hit the one-ball. To find this initial target region, the player stands behind the cue ball to eye up the various paths the cue ball could take which will strike the one-ball. As indicated in Fig. 3.4, the first part of the scenario defines a fairly large target region on the cue ball; it is indicated by the larger arc near the cue ball.

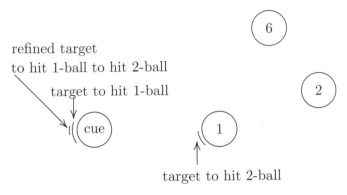

**Fig. 3.4.** A pool shot

But the cue ball hitting the one-ball is only the first part of the desired action. After all, the goal is to hit the one-ball in a manner so that it will hit the two-ball. To determine this "target region" on the one-ball, the player walks around the table and carefully eyes up how the one-ball and two-ball are positioned.

After determining a target region on the one-ball (see Fig. 3.4), the player returns to the cue ball to refine its target area. This refined target area — the smaller arc near the cue ball in the figure — is where to strike the cue ball so it will hit the targeted region on the one-ball which hits the two-ball. This continued refinement process continues; the target region on the two-ball generates a refined target region on the one-ball which creates a refined region on the cue ball.

There are two ways to use this construction. The first is to compute the precise location of the striking point; quite frankly, this can be difficult work requiring the expertise of a Fast Eddie or a Willie Mosconi. The second, more relaxed approach is to determine whether it is possible to make the described shot. The advantage of the second approach is that rather than finding precise initial striking locations, we just need to determine whether it is possible for someone, maybe a Minnesota Fats, to make a shot where each successive stage of the story occurs. The tradeoff for precision is the ability to discover all possible actions; namely, by emphasizing what can occur, it may become possible to catalogue everything that can occur.

To explain, the above story describes only one scenario; another scenario might be to determine whether it is possible for the "one-ball to hit the six-ball to hit the three-ball to hit the two-ball which goes in the near pocket." In Fig. 3.4, this difference starts by finding where to hit the one-ball so that it hits the six ball; this defines a different target region on the one-ball and then a different region on the cue ball. But the arrangements of the balls might make it impossible for the six-ball to hit the three-ball. If so, then any description involving such a sequence is impossible. In other words, by emphasizing and understanding how this "refined targeting" approach works, by recognizing obstacles which prevent certain sequencing, it may be possible to catalogue all possible events that could occur.

Of course, the cue ball analysis allows only a finite number of steps; problems for dynamics typically involve an infinite number of them. Here, mathematical tools are developed to determine all possible ways this refined targeting approach can be developed. In other words, those mathematical terms such as "homoclinic points," "horse shoe maps" and so forth are mathematical constructs which indirectly ensure that each of many initial target regions can be refined into a large number of other target regions allowing a more complicated future, and each of these refined target regions can be further refined ... This refinement of refinements continues infinitely long.

By the way, this pool hall story explains the familiar "sensitivity with respect to initial conditions" phrase. To carry out the desired itinerary of "this ball hits that ball hits the other ball," a precise target region is identified on the cue ball. If the player is ever so slightly off, the resulting consequence can be radically different from that which was planned.

**4.2. Back to voting, and other aggregation methods.** At least conceptually, the approach to identify all possible voting paradoxes follows this iterated "refined targeting" philosophy. For voting, the "target region" is the space of profiles; it is the space of all possible ways different voters can rank the candidates. The action of the cue stick and the initial arrangement of the balls is represented by the specified voting procedures. The itinerary of possible dynamical behavior is is given by the possible lists of the election rankings of different subsets of the candidates.

All earlier attempts used in the field to discover what could happen in elections were akin to the pool hall approach of finding the precise location where to hit the cue ball. Just as hitting the cue ball to deliver a desired, complicated outcome requires the skills of a Fast Eddie, the earlier attempts to construct a specific illustrating example proved to be difficult. The reasons are clear; first, the combinatorics needed to design a profile or example can be complicated. This complexity severely limited the scope of earlier examples. Even more difficult was the need to guess what to look for; it involved a search "for what unexpected election outcome do I think I can find an illustrating example?" Quite clearly, this approach never would suffice to identify all "unexpected, unanticipated behaviors."

Thus, to tackle the more general project, my goal was not to find actual examples illustrating any specified listing of election rankings (however, that now is possible to do). Instead, my goal was to modify this refined, iterated targeting approach, illustrated by the pool hall story, in a way which could identify when one kind of an election ranking can, or cannot, accompany some other kind of election ranking.

To suggest how this can be done, start with the set of all candidates. There are many ways to rank these candidates; these different ranking divide the space of all possible profiles into "target regions." Namely, each target region consists of all possible profiles which give rise the specified election outcome. For instance, one "target region" consists of all possible profiles which would lead to a plurality $A \succ C \succ D \succ B \succ E$ ranking, another target region would lead to a $A \approx B \succ E \succ C \approx D$ plurality outcome, and so forth.

Guided by the approach from dynamics, the next step is to consider what can happen when $E$ drops out. As with the pool hall story, the goal is to understand whether each of the first regions can be further subdivided to allow, say, a $C \succ A \succ B \succ D$, or a $D \succ A \approx C \succ B$, or a ... Again, rather than carrying out actual computations, which would quickly overwhelm even the fastest computer or the most patient mathematician, emphasis is placed on obstacles; what prevents target regions from being refined? This process is continued; can these refined target regions be further subdivided to handle different rankings when $C$, instead of $E$ drops out?

While I used a fairly direct modification of this approach from dynamics to obtain my first results in this direction (e.g., [**40**]), it quickly became clear that the approach was overly labor intensive; what was particularly troubling was that the labor was mine! Consequently, again following the lead of dynamical systems, indirect means of determining what can happen needed to be developed; in this way the more general results were discovered and proved. Nevertheless, this iterated "targeting" approach more accurately describes why the results occur.

There remains the question of understanding why some some voting methods allow all sorts of paradoxes while others do not. The explanation comes again from that pool hall. Remember that "the one-ball hits the two-ball hits the three-ball ... " scenario? Maybe this shot is impossible to make. After all, the initial arrangement of the balls might be such that it is impossible to find a target region on the one-ball which will allow it to hit the two-ball. Similarly, the structure of certain voting methods prohibits certain arrangements of rankings. For instance, if $A$ is the Condorcet winner (so she beats all other candidates in pairwise votes) while $E$ is the Condorcet loser, this targeting approach shows it is impossible to have a Borda Count ranking where $E$ is ranked above $A$; this Borda voting approach is too selective and restrictive. But all other positional procedures have enough flexibility to allow this contradictory behavior.

**4.3. The "almost all" structure.** The collection of those rare voting procedures define something which is mathematically called a "proper algebraic variety" with a "stratified structure." To describe these terms in more common language, imagine the hierarchical power structure of a religious or political organization. Start, for instance, with a parliamentary system of voters. Here, some voters are "more equal" than others because they are members of parliament. Then, one parliament member is "more equal" than others by being the prime minister. Similarly, in a church hierarchy, there are the faithful. Among the faithful are the ministers. "More equal" among the ministers are the Bishops.

To give this stratification term a geometric story, suppose the goal is to identify a particular point in a cube. First consider the front face; this defines a boundary of the cube. Next, consider the top edge; this is one the boundaries of the front face. Finally consider the vertex on the right-hand side; it is one the boundaries of the top edge. This setting, where a region is in the boundary of the previous region, is the "more equal" stratification notion needed here.

To describe the hierarchy of voting procedures, the singular voting method playing the role of the above vertex is the "Borda Count." Much like building a child's pinwheel, there are several lines of lists of voting procedures (where the line is defined by adjusting certain tallying weights) which all connect at the Borda Count; the BC is on the boundary of all of these lines. The BC is "more equal" than any of these voting procedures on the line in the sense that it is strong enough to avoid certain voting paradoxes; it is the prime minister. In other words, any example someone can construct which displays a weird, unexpected listing of BC voting rankings also displays problems that can occur with any of these other procedures. However, each of these other procedures is not sufficiently strong to avoid other kinds of paradoxes; they allow examples of unexpected rankings over different subsets of candidates that never can occur with the BC.

So far, this description has the members of parliament — the voting methods which define lines — and the prime minister — the BC. Next, we come to the citizens. Think of these as two-dimensional collections of voting procedures as defined by the different weights. The boundaries of these sheets are the earlier lines of voting methods. Again, each method on the sheet suffers the precise problems of the unexpected election rankings experienced by the methods on the lines. However, the methods on the sheets allow even more troubling voting problems.

This construction continues; the sheets turn out to be boundaries for three-dimensional sets of procedures. The same hierarchy of voting problems extends. Then, the three-dimensional sets are the boundaries for four-dimensional sets of voting procedures. All of this continues until we arrive at the general setting where the extra procedures allow anything to occur. Unfortunately for the way in which we conduct the business of democracy, this set of voting methods includes the plurality vote as well as all of those commonly used "vote for $k$ candidates" methods. It also includes the component parts of Approval and Cumulative Voting.

# Chapter 4

# How to Be Strategic

Be honest. At times you have voted strategically. I sure have. The 2000 election was full of examples where voters voted for someone other than their favored choice to try to force a personally more preferred election result. The most notable example is where Nader voters in hotly contested states promised to vote for Gore — to try to avoid a Bush victory — if a Gore voter from a state safely in Gore's column would vote for Nader. Without question, both voters were voting strategically. As another example, during the Michigan presidential primary the governor of Michigan failed on his promise to deliver his state's Republican primary vote for George W. Bush. His excuse was that the winner, John McCain, won only by strategically attracting cross-over votes of Independents and Democrats.

Strategic voting is a reality; it occurs in our social groups, in our workplace, in the judging of events such as figure skating, and in our elections. But how and when can it be done? Can it be avoided? To examine these issues, I use mathematics to explain how to identify when and how an election outcome can be strategically altered.

Before doing so, let me repeat a disclaimer from a *Math Horizons* article.[1] My intent is not to train a generation of manipulative strategists — the game theorists and economists do a better job of this. Instead, I want to alert the reader to subtle political actions which can, and do, affect us.

---

[1] Along with the disclaimer, some of the material in this chapter is modification of an article (Saari [**58**]) the editors of *Math Horizons* asked me to write. I thank the editors, Deanna Haunsperger and Steve Kennedy, and the Mathematical Association of America for permission to use this material which appeared in the November 2000 issue.

Each of the three main components of an election — the procedure, voting, and process — offers manipulative opportunities. To be manipulative, anticipate strategic opportunities to arise whenever a setting, or a slight change, generates several different election outcomes. Then design a strategy to force the personally preferred choice.

## 1. Choice of a procedure

Most people do not care about the choice of an election procedure. The cost of their ignorance is that they are unaware of how the approach can drastically change the outcome. As we learned (e.g., Thm. 3 on page 37), a single profile can generate a surprisingly large number of different election outcomes. The several available outcomes invite manipulative behavior. The strategy is obvious; check whether some procedure provides a personally better outcome; if so, then promote that method.

To review how the choice of a voting procedure matters, consider the following profile for the three candidates Alice, Barb, and Carole.

(22)

| Number | Preference | Number | Preference |
|--------|------------|--------|------------|
| 6 | $A \succ B \succ C$ | 7 | $C \succ B \succ A$ |
| 5 | $A \succ C \succ B$ | | |

The procedure line for this 18-voter profile, as illustrated in Fig. 4.1, proves that each candidate "wins" with an appropriate voting method. For our purposes, it suffices to note just three special cases.

- *Alice* wins by a plurality landslide by receiving over 61% of the plurality vote. Her solid victory makes it seem hopeless to try to elect somebody else. But this is not true.

- *Barb* wins with the antiplurality vote. Recall, this is where the voters vote *against* somebody in the socially acceptable manner of voting *for* two candidates. Thus, the $B \succ C \succ A$ outcome shows that Alice is bottom ranked by many of these voters.

- *Carole* wins with $\mathbf{w}_{5/6}$; this is equivalent to assigning 6 and 5 points, respectively, to a voter's first and second choices. The $C \succ A \succ B$ outcome has a 67: 66: 65 tally.

While this profile illustrates again that an election outcome can reflect the choice of an election procedure rather than the voters' views, *it also identifies strategic opportunities for a young aspiring Machiavelli to select a procedure which yields his preferred winner.* It also carries a somewhat ominous message; even if a candidate's support is in the landslide category (Alice is top ranked by over 60% of the voters), manipulative opportunities still may exist.

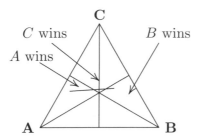

**Fig. 4.1.** Strategies from procedure line; Eq. 22

If our Machiavelli wants Alice to win, he should support the use of the standard plurality vote. For Barb's victory, emphasize the virtues of the antiplurality vote — the need to "worry about who voters dislike." This is the "Let's start by seeing who we should drop" attitude which is familiar to anyone who has ever served on a personnel committee. For Carole's victory, Machiavelli should fashion an argument describing why imposing a slight distinction between a first- and second-ranked candidate — given by the 6, 5, 0, point approach — is better than the antiplurality approach. So, to manipulate the outcome our Machiavelli just needs to devise a passable story promoting a preferred method. This is not a difficult challenge.

Our Machiavelli, of course, needs to select the appropriate procedure — the appropriate choice of "$s$" for $\mathbf{w}_s = (1, s, 0)$ — for a specified profile. But this requires doing nothing more than constructing the procedure line as described on page 46. As the Fig. 4.1 procedure line displays, even a seemingly innocuous profile where Alice appears to be the undisputed winner[2] can generate seven different election outcomes where anyone can be elected. With more than three alternatives, the strategic choice of a procedure follows from the construction of the procedure simplex.

A remaining concern is whether only rare, unlikely instances of voter preferences allow the election ranking to switch with the choice of weights. But, as already described, Maria Tataru and I proved [**64**] that even with conservative assumptions about the distribution of voters' preferences, about 69% of the three-candidate profiles allow the election ranking to change with the weights. More candidates provide more strategic opportunities. When pairwise voting methods and methods such as runoffs are included, the likelihood of changing an outcome with the procedure increases.

Incidentally, strategic behavior extends beyond voting. Later (Chapter 6) when I briefly describe other aggregation methods, it will become clear

---

[2]The voters never will know this. Seldom does anybody check actual preferences; the most that is done is to check voting tallies.

that the statistical approaches, power indices, and all sorts of approaches also can be manipulated.

## 2. Strategic voting

As we cannot continually change the election procedure, the next step is to examine how to be strategic in the privacy of the voting booth. Quite frankly, this is commonly done.

After the Michigan 2000 primaries, for instance, a Keyes' supporter confided that since Keyes had no realistic chance of winning, he strategically voted for Bush to try to prevent McCain from winning. As another example, the earlier described Doonesbury cartoon strip (page 17) could be interpreted as encouraging Nader voters to strategically vote for Gore in the November 2000 election.

A problem with this commonly used "Don't waste your vote!" strategy is that it alters the legitimacy of any message based on election outcomes. As such, it is worth trying to invent a procedure where it never is in a voter's best interest to be strategic. Surely the power of mathematics can be used to devise such an approach.

**2.1. The Gibbard-Satterthwaite Theorem.** No such method exists. In the early 1970s, Allan Gibbard, at the University of Michigan, and Mark Satterthwaite, at Northwestern University, independently proved the remarkable result that, with three or more alternatives, all reasonable election procedures (e.g., no dictators) provide opportunities for someone to strategically obtain a personally more favorable outcome.

**Theorem 8** (Gibbard [**19**], Satterthwaite [**68**]). *If there are three or more candidates where each candidate can be the winner, and if the procedure is not a dictatorship, then situations exist where it is in the best interest of some voter to vote strategically rather than sincerely.*

The large literature describing and extending this result can be difficult to read. But, by knowing that the Gibbard-Satterthwaite Theorem holds, the result becomes fairly easy to understand, extend, and reprove.

With only two candidates, say Sandra and Theresa, the voter is virtuous — not by intent, but by the lack of opportunities as the only outcomes are

Sandra wins, or Theresa wins.

If you prefer Sandra, then you have to vote sincerely for her. But with more candidates, there are more outcomes. The richer list of possibilities creates a temptation to be strategic to enjoy certain newly available opportunities. For instance, should Robin join the race, then (ignoring ties) the three possible results,

Robin wins,  Sandra wins,  or Theresa wins,

suggest that a situation can occur — as the Gibbard-Satterthewaite Theorem claims — where our voter who prefers Sandra but dislikes Theresa is better off voting strategically for Robin. For instance, a situation may occur where a voter preferring Nader should vote for Gore. This assertion holds independent of the procedure as long as a voter's vote can affect the outcome.

Election rankings introduce even more tempting options. With the three candidates, the three rankings (ignoring ties) where Sandra is preferred to Theresa are

1. Sandra $\succ$ Robin $\succ$ Theresa,

2. Robin $\succ$ Sandra $\succ$ Theresa, and

3. Sandra $\succ$ Theresa $\succ$ Robin.

So, our voter preferring Sandra to Theresa can target his vote to enhance the likelihood of any of these outcomes. The exact choice depends on the circumstances; our strategic voter needs to examine the different options to determine which one leads to a personally more favored outcome.

The proof of the Gibbard-Satterthwaite Theorem follows from these simple notions. The extra candidate introduces new directions for the election outcome. When the tallies are near a tie, then, with so many different types of voters, it has to be in *some* voter's personal interest to vote strategically.

**2.2. When strategies work.** While the Gibbard-Satterthwaite result ensures that all voting procedures offer strategic opportunities for our Machiavelli, the theorem does not explain how to recognize when they arise or how to take advantage of them. Not much help comes from the extensive literature which favors existence theorems — proving that strategic opportunities exist — over the pragmatic issue of finding them. So, what are these strategic opportunities?

Common sense dictates that if a single voter can change the outcome, the sincere outcome must be close to a tie. While it is rare for a profile to have a nearly tied outcome, they exist; the 2000 presidential election is a prime example. Yet, it is clear that had, say, the Borda Count been used in the 2000 election, the outcome would not have been so close. This suggests, and it is true, that

- a profile which offers strategic opportunities for one method need not offer strategic opportunities for another, and

- not all procedures are equally manipulable; some procedures offer more strategic opportunities than others.

While results furthering these comments are described later, let me illustrate them by using the candidates {Anni, Brigid, Carola} and by comparing the strategic opportunities which occur with the plurality vote and with Approval Voting. For a voter to have a strategic chance with the plurality vote, the two top candidates, say Anni and Brigid, must be essentially tied. This can occur, but such profiles are relatively rare.

Strategic opportunities for AV, on the other hand, accompany most profiles. To see this, suppose Anni is the plurality winner; she could even win by a landslide 60% of the vote. (So no voter has a strategic opportunity with this plurality vote.) All that is required for AV to admit strategic settings

> is for enough voters to have either Brigid or Carola *second ranked* so that the total of their first *and* second place votes is larger than Anni's *first place votes.*

Whenever a profile satisfies this requirement, its AV hull positions many admissible AV outcomes near one of the "tied election" lines. (See Sect. 2.4 and Fig. 4.2.) Each point creates a strategic situation promised by the Gibbard-Satterthwaite Theorem.

All sorts of profiles admit AV strategic opportunites. Indeed, a profile always does so unless it essentially reduces to a two-candidate election. An instructive way to see this is to accept my challenge to prove me wrong. That is, by using the Fig. 2.1 approach of representing profiles, try to create a profile which is not, essentially, a de facto two-person race and where the sum of the first- and second-place votes for Brigid and for Carola both are smaller than Anni's first-place vote. What will cause frustration is that someone who ranks Anni in top place also ranks another candidates in second place.

**2.3. The math societies' election procedure.** If all procedures can be manipulated, then it is worth worrying more about the one adopted by the Mathematics Association of American and the American Mathematical Society. As shown above, if an election is not, essentially, a two-candidate race, AV will offer a surprising number of manipulative opportunities. But what are they?

To outline what can happen, the shaded area of Fig. 4.2 represents a typical portion of a profile's possible AV election outcomes. The arrows indicate how an outcome changes if a new voter joins; e.g., a scalar multiple of the arrow pointing downwards indicates how the outcome would change if a voter votes for both $A$ and $B$; a multiple of the arrow pointing toward the south-east is the change in the outcome should a voter vote only for $B$.

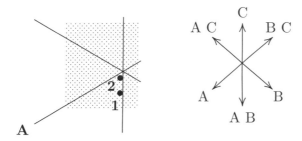

**Fig. 4.2.** AV strategies

The two bullets isolate two possible "$A \succ B \succ C$" AV election outcomes near a tie vote, so both invite strategic action. The analysis involves nothing more than figuring which of the six directions represented by the arrows you would prefer to use to move the election outcome — a specified bullet. Then mark the ballot accordingly.

To illustrate with the first outcome (bullet #1), suppose you prefer $C \succ B \succ A$ and you only want to vote for $C$. According to the figure, as this sincere vote moves the election outcome (bullet #1) directly upwards, *it helps to elect your bottom choice of A.* According to the figure, the only way to avoid this frightful outcome is to vote strategically to move the outcome to the right. According to the arrows, the only two strategic options are to vote only for $B$, or to vote for $B$ and $C$.

By applying this same, simple geometric argument to each type of voter, we can characterize, as done next, all possible ways to be strategic. In this table, the "Sincere" column lists how the voter would sincerely mark the ballot; for instance, the $AB$ listed for a type one voter in the "Sincere" column means that this voter would sincerely vote for both candidates. The adjacent column, listed as "strategic," describes how this voter should vote to move the bullet in a desired direction. Of course, for some voters, a sincere vote may be the optimal one. When this is true, a "$S$" in the *Strategic* column means "a sincere vote."

(23)

| Type | Sincere | Strategic | Sincere | Strategic |
|------|---------|-----------|---------|-----------|
| 1 | $AB$ | $A, AC$ | $A$ | $S, AC$ |
| 2 | $AC$ | $S, A$ | $A$ | $S, AC$ |
| 3 | $CA$ | $S, C, A$ | $C$ | $S, A, AC$ |
| 4 | $CB$ | $S, B$ | $C$ | $B$ |
| 5 | $BC$ | $S, B$ | $B$ | $S$ |
| 6 | $BA$ | $B, BC$ | $B$ | $S, BC$ |

**Strategies for the #1 AV outcome**

The second AV outcome, bullet #2, has a $A \succ B \succ C$ outcome which is close to a complete tie. The associated strategies follow.

|     | Type | Sincere | Strategic | Sincere | Strategic |
|-----|------|---------|-----------|---------|-----------|
|     | 1    | $AB$    | $A$       | $A$     | $S$       |
|     | 2    | $AC$    | $S, C$    | $A$     | $S$       |
| (24) | 3   | $CA$    | $S, C$    | $C$     | $S$       |
|     | 4    | $CB$    | $S, B$    | $C$     | $BC$      |
|     | 5    | $BC$    | $S, B$    | $B$     | $S$       |
|     | 6    | $BA$    | $B$       | $B$     | $S$       |

**Strategies for the #2 AV outcome**

To illustrate, again suppose you are a type-four voter ($C \succ B \succ A$ preferences) who strongly prefers $C$; a sincere vote moves the outcome upwards into the $A \succ C \succ B$ region where $A$ still wins. A preferred choice is to move the outcome to the right; namely, strategically voting for $B$, or for both $B$ and $C$, helps to elect $B$ rather than $A$.

All of the potential strategic opportunities, as characterized in Fig. 4.2, suggest why AV encourages strategic voting. For a practical verification, recall my earlier comments (page 53) about the 1999 Social Choice and Welfare Society AV election which involved three candidates so highly regarded that, most surely, most (if not all) voters sincerely approved of more than one of them. But as an election with popular, well-qualified candidates would be closely contested, the obvious AV strategy (as verified by the above tables) was to vote for one candidate. Thus, a reasonable measure of the voters' strategic intent was to determine the percentage of voters doing so. Before the actual election, I wildly predicted that over half, maybe even 65%, would vote for only one candidate. Was I wrong! As only one voter from the Fig. 2.7a data voted for more than one candidate, it was about 98%! The message is that in a competitive election, expect AV to revert to the plurality voting system — a system AV was intended to replace.

Although it is rarely used in actual elections, there are other examples verifying the adoption of the above AV strategic approaches. In particular, expect strategic attitudes to force AV back into a plurality vote. This happened when AV was used in a 1984 election for the Democratic party in Pennsylvania. As U.S. Senator Terry Sanford (when he was president of Duke University) noted, "The great weakness, it seemed to me, was that most voters ... are inclined to cheat a little and 'single shot' if it suits their purposes, which it generally does. I was present for the Pennsylvania straw vote, helped to explain it, and was not surprised when very few who voted for [candidate A] voted for anyone else, although surely there were other acceptable candidates."[3]

As a final example, long before I studied voting systems and discovered many worrisome AV properties, I was sufficiently intrigued by AV to support its use to elect the committee to select the new president for Northwestern University. The chair of another department asked, "Did you see the silly election procedure? Is it easy to manipulate!" His strategy was for his department to propose some candidates, for the math department to propose others; with both departments voting just for these candidates, we could determine the committee. I leave it to you to wonder whether we did this.

**2.4. Different procedures.** The Fig. 4.2 geometry captures the essence of the Gibbard-Satterthwaite Theorem while indicating how to find strategic choices. To review in directional terms, a two-person election becomes an "east-west" choice. If I want to go east, I have no options; I must vote for "east." More candidates, however, introduce more directions. Although I still want to go east, maneuvering to go "north-east" is preferred to going west. Indeed, a way to verify the Gibbard-Satterthwaite Theorem is to show how their conditions admit the extra directions and flexibility so that we can mimic the above directional geometry.

At this point it would be natural to describe strategic actions for all procedures. But the description is a bit technical, so it is left for the last section of this chapter. Instead, since some methods offer more strategic opportunities than others, it is reasonable to wonder which positional methods are most susceptible to manipulative behavior. The following theorem gives the surprising answer; technical details are left to the references.

**Theorem 9** (Saari, [**42, 49**]). *Suppose only a small percentage of the voters are trying to be strategic in a three-candidate election. The procedures which are most susceptible to a successful manipulation are the plurality and antiplurality votes. The unique procedure which is least susceptible to a successful manipulation is the Borda Count.*

To provide intuition for this result, remember that opportunities for a successful manipulation require a nearly tied vote. So part of the proof involves determining which procedure has the smallest number of nearly tied outcomes. This is the Borda Count. Conversely, the plurality and antiplurality vote have the largest number nearly tied outcomes.

As a way to explain this phenomenon, recall those problems asking to find the rectangle with a fixed area and the smallest perimeter. The answer is the most symmetric rectangle — a square. Similarly, the ellipse with a

---

[3]Personal letter to D. G. Saari, dated 19 April 1985.

fixed area and the smallest circumference is a circle. In general, the more symmetric the object, the smaller the surface area.

A similar construct occurs in voting. All positional methods have a sixth of the profiles defining, say, the $A \succ B \succ C$ outcome. So expect the most symmetric voting method to have the smallest boundary — hence the fewest strategic opportunities. This symmetric method is the Borda Count; the BC has a fixed difference between the number of points given to a first- and second-, and a second- and third-ranked candidates. The methods with the largest boundary should be the ones furthest from symmetry — the plurality and antiplurality methods. This intuition captures precisely what happens.

## 3. Debate and selecting amendments

To underscore the worrisome fact that election outcomes can radically vary with the choice of a procedure, I often joke during lectures that

> *"For a price, I will serve as a consultant for your group for your next election. Tell me who you want to win. After talking to the members of your organization, I will design a 'democratic procedure' which ensures the election of your candidate."*[4]

To demonstrate that my joke goes beyond bad humor to be a realistic warning, suppose a 30-member department is evenly split over the eight candidates for a tenure-track position; 10 each prefer

$$\begin{aligned} A &\succ B \succ \mathbf{C} \succ D \succ E \succ F \succ G \succ \mathbf{H}, \\ B &\succ \mathbf{C} \succ D \succ E \succ F \succ G \succ \mathbf{H} \succ A, \\ \mathbf{C} &\succ D \succ E \succ F \succ G \succ \mathbf{H} \succ A \succ B. \end{aligned}$$

(25)

$C$ appears to be the departmental favorite; only she is highly ranked by all voters. $H$, on the other hand, is so poorly appreciated that *all* voters prefer $C$, $D$, $E$, $F$, and even $G$ to $H$. The challenge is to elect $H$ with a procedure which involves all candidates and where all voters are satisfied that $H$ truly reflects the departmental wishes. Let me encourage you to try to design such a method before reading any further.

**3.1. Electing the unelectable.** It is easy to elect $C$; just use the Borda Count. While it appears to be a serious challenge to elect $H$, the approach actually is simple; just use an appropriate agenda where the winning candidate in each pairing is advanced to be compared with the next candidate.

For instance, in the agenda depicted in Fig. 4.3 (purposely placed on the next page), the first election is between $G$ and $F$. But, *everyone* prefers $F$ to $G$, so the unanimous choice $F$ is advanced to be compared with $E$.

---

[4]Please, no calls, no letters, no offers. This is only a joke!

Of course, as *everyone* in the above profile prefers $E$ to $F$, $E$ is advanced to be compared with $D$. Then $D$ with $C$. When $C$ is compared with $B$, two-thirds of these voters prefer $B$. The story continues — with $H$ being the winner.

As true with basketball tournaments, the strategic action involves the seeding. The seeded agenda of Fig. 4.3 not only elects $H$, but as each election outcome is decided either unanimously or by a landslide two-thirds vote, it is unlikely for anyone to object. After all, what we usually know about the preferences of others is what is revealed in an election. So, while each and every person in this group will leave the meeting unhappy about the conclusion, nobody is likely to fault the procedure. What a mistake.

**3.2. Not in my group!** The smug reader may feel confident that his or her organization is immune to this strategic behavior if only because their decisions are made in an open manner with full discussions and by consensus. Think again; this bothersome phenomena can fully arise even during a friendly discussion.

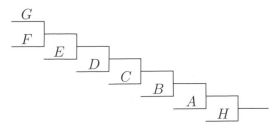

**Figure 4.3.** Designing a manipulative agenda

To illustrate, think back to a recent departmental meeting called to select a new calculus book where someone suggested book $G$ only to have it compared with $F$. As everyone prefers the graphics in $F$, $G$ is dismissed without a vote. But $F$ is heavy while book $E$ will not induce hernias by lugging it to class, so the discussion shifts from $F$ to $E$.

The debate continues by covering one detail after another; $D$ handles the limit process better than $E$; $C$ describes derivatives more intuitively than $D$, and so forth. At each stage, the strong support for the new alternative makes votes unnecessary. The result? Inferior $H$ wins with such a strong consensus that a vote never is necessary. This problem of "selecting a poor choice" is inherent in the dynamics of the discussion; the sad fact is that the organization may never recognize why they made such an inferior choice.

**3.3. Opportunities for Machiavelli.** The opportunities for our young Machiavelli come from governing the dynamics of the discussion, by finding ways to compare stronger competitors at an early stage to eliminate them.

But, always, always, try to introduce your personally desired choice at the end of the discussion. I will return to this behavior in the next section.

If a group is unanimous in their belief, then surely it is impossible to strategically elect the bottom-ranked candidate while keeping all voters content. Or is it? Suppose the above example started with everyone preferring

$$C \succ D \succ E \succ F \succ G \succ H.$$

To elect $H$, in addition to finding the correct seeding, just introduce two amendments $A$ and $B$ which divide the voters as above. Yes, this is more involved, but to solve the "impossible," we should try harder.

## 4. Any relief?

While strategic voting never will be eliminated, some of its effects can be reduced. However, as a word of caution, never adopt a procedure which is relatively strategy-proof without first checking the merits of its sincere outcomes. For instance, it is easy to create a fully strategy-proof approach — a dictatorship. Although free from manipulative schemes, I doubt I would embrace the procedure's "sincere" outcomes — unless I can be the dictator.

The key point to remember is that a strategic voter is not voting as he or she sincerely believes. Thus, strategic voting is risky because the final outcome might reflect how you voted rather than your intended strategic gains. This means that a strategic voter needs to know

- how do the other voters plan to vote, and
- how will my strategic intentions — the way I mark my ballot — move the final outcome.

Stated in another manner, successful strategic voting involves assembling considerable information.

Partial remedies are immediate. Think of a snowy February in New Hampshire when voters are reviewing the Presidential candidates.

"I want to vote for John, but the polls in the paper suggest
that if I do, then Roger will get elected instead of Alice."

Election polls can encourage manipulative behavior. They provide the information needed to make the calculations as to whether a strategic vote will be helpful, or harmful.

How do we get around this? I really don't have a full answer. France and other countries prohibit the publishing of polling information for a specified period just prior to certain elections. While that helps, it is not clear how effective such an approach will be now that the polls could be published in other countries and made available on the internet.

Perhaps we should design approaches where it is easy to vote sincerely, but overly complicated to successfully vote strategically. One way to increase the strategic computations is to use runoffs — but not where voters can cast ballots in each election. After all, in a standard runoff, our Machiavelli would vote to advance a weak opponent into the runoff; in the runoff, he would vote for his first choice. But, if Machiavelli's votes at all stages are determined in advance — always by the original way the ballots are marked as true with the Instant Runoff Procedure — then the manipulative opportunities are significantly reduced. They are not eliminated, but they are not as obvious.

What would I recommend? I would avoid changing procedures with each election. Then, to combine the consistency of Borda outcomes while frustrating manipulative voting, I would use an "Instant Borda Runoff." This means (as suggested by E. J. Nanson [33] ) that the candidates are first ranked with a Borda Count; the bottom candidate is dropped, and the remaining candidates are reranked with the Borda Count. This continues until one candidate — the winner — remains. But, each voter submits only one listing of the candidates; this listing is used for each election.

Other approaches depend on the setting. For instance, a de facto runoff occurs during every primary season. This is true for the Presidential primaries, those for senator, maybe representative, or even the local dog catcher. The obvious strategy is to vote in the "other party's primary" to help elect a weaker opponent. Once this strategy is understood, a natural corrective action is to limit primary voting only to voters registered in that party.

The main point is that by knowing the mathematical source of strategic action, it is possible to construct corrective action. It mainly requires some imagination.

## 5. Changing the outcome

In this concluding section of the chapter, I become slightly more technical to suggest how to formalize the Fig. 4.2 type notions to develop a way to find all strategies for all procedures. (The reader who has yet to embrace the delights of vector calculus, or who gets bogged down in the notation should skip ahead to the next chapter.) In doing so, I use the vector representation of a profile introduced on page 42.

To illustrate the use of the vector notation, when Bob, a type-four voter, votes as though he is type six, there is one less type-four voter and one more type-six voter. This change is represented by vector $\mathbf{v} = (0, 0, 0, -1, 0, 1)$. Notice that the $-1$ means Bob no longer votes as though type four while the $+1$ represents Bob's actual voting approach. If the original profile is $\mathbf{p}$, the profile adjusted by Bob's action is $\mathbf{p} + \mathbf{v}$.

Let $f(\mathbf{p})$ be the election procedure which determines the winner (or election ranking) for profile $\mathbf{p}$. The electoral difference Bob caused by adjusting the profile is

$$(26) \qquad\qquad\qquad f(\mathbf{p} + \mathbf{v}) - f(\mathbf{p}).$$

Unfortunately, Eq. 26 does not make sense. For instance, if $f(\mathbf{p} + \mathbf{v}) = \{\text{Gore}\}$ and $f(\mathbf{p}) = \{\text{Bush}\}$, what does $f(\mathbf{p}+\mathbf{v}) - f(\mathbf{p}) = \{\text{Gore}\} - \{\text{Bush}\}$ mean? While the 2000 election and its aftermath make it particularly tempting to explore the differences between these candidates, return to mathematics by noticing how, at least formally, Eq. 26 resembles the start of the definition for a gradient and directional derivative

$$(27) \qquad\qquad\qquad f(\mathbf{p} + \mathbf{v}) - f(\mathbf{p}) \approx \nabla f(\mathbf{p}) \cdot \mathbf{v}.$$

To convert this nonsensical expression into a useful tool, note that $f^{-1}(\text{Gore})$ and $f^{-1}(\text{Bush})$ are defined; they represent all profiles which elect, respectively, Gore and Bush. So, if Bob's actions, $\mathbf{v}$, change the election outcome, then $\mathbf{v}$ crosses a boundary separating these two profile sets.

If the gradient, $\nabla f$, did exist, it would define a vector orthogonal to a $f$ level set which points in the direction of greatest change. This suggests replacing $\nabla f$ in Eq. 27 with a normal vector $\mathbf{N}$ to this separating boundary. Since this "boundary" consists of the profiles where the two candidates are tied (if they exist), we return to the "nearly tied" comments made earlier.

If this normal vector $\mathbf{N}$ points into the set which elects Gore, then, if

$$(28) \qquad\qquad \mathbf{N} \cdot \mathbf{v} \text{ is } \begin{cases} > 0, & \text{the change helps Gore,} \\ < 0, & \text{the change helps Bush,} \\ = 0, & \text{the change is neutral.} \end{cases}$$

In other words, a loose but useful interpretation of Eq. 27 is that the sign of $\mathbf{N} \cdot \mathbf{v}$ indicates the potential change in the election outcome; this algebra replaces the "arrows" and geometric reasoning of Fig. 4.2.

To review, a profile $\mathbf{p}$ can be strategically manipulated if $\mathbf{p}$ is sufficiently close to a tie vote so that a voter can change the outcome. A useful strategy is a $\mathbf{v}$ which changes the outcome in a desired manner. To illustrate the use of this tool, I calculate the strategies which change the $\{A, B\}$ ranking of a $\mathbf{w}_s$ election.

The boundary separating where $A$ and $B$ wins is the profiles which define a $A \approx B$ tie. $A$'s tally for profile $\mathbf{p} = (p_1, \dots, p_6)$ is $p_1 + p_2 + sp_3 + sp_6$, $B$'s tally is $p_5 + p_6 + sp_1 + sp_4$, so a $A \approx B$ tie requires the two tallies to agree, or

$$[p_1 + p_2 + sp_3 + sp_6] - [p_5 + p_6 + sp_1 + sp_4]$$
$$= (1 - s)p_1 + p_2 + sp_3 - sp_4 - p_5 + (s - 1)p_6 = 0.$$

Notice how this expression captures my earlier comment that the profiles which allow a strategic setting can change with the procedure. For instance, the plurality vote has $s = 0$, so all profiles near

$$[p_1 + p_2] - [p_5 + p_6] = 0$$

qualify. For the antiplurality vote, with $s = 1$, the qualifying condition is that the profile nearly satisfies the quite different condition of

$$[p_1 + p_2 + p_3 + p_6] - [p_5 + p_6 + p_1 + p_4] = 0.$$

To find a normal vector $\mathbf{N}$, treat $p_j$ as a real variable rather than a nonnegative integer. The gradient of the above expression defines the normal vector

$$\mathbf{N}_s = ((1-s), 1, s, -s, -1, -(1-s))$$

which points toward those profiles which help candidate $A$

This $\mathbf{N}_s$ makes it easy to determine who can be Machiavellian. Clearly, the type one, two and three voters, who prefer $A$ to $B$, have no interest in assisting $B$. If a type-four voter wants to change this $A \succ B$ outcome, then the change vector $\mathbf{v}$ has $-1$ in the fourth component reflecting that he no longer votes sincerely. The voter's strategy — the way he actually votes — determines which $\mathbf{v}$ coordinate has $+1$. Remember, to help $B$, this voter's strategy must ensure that $\mathbf{N}_s \cdot \mathbf{v} < 0$.

As $\mathbf{v}$ has only two non-zero terms, a "+1" and a "−1," the dot product changes the sign of $\mathbf{N}_s$'s fourth coordinate to $s$ and adds it to the $\mathbf{N}_s$ coordinate which represents the voter's strategy. So, finding a successful strategy reduces to finding $\mathbf{N}_s$ components which are less than $-s$. If our Machiavelli votes as though type six, so $\mathbf{v} = (0, 0, 0, -1, 0, 1)$, the dot product of $s - (1-s) = 2s - 1$ certifies this strategy as useful (i.e., $\mathbf{N}_s \cdot \mathbf{v} < 0$) if and only if the procedure is defined by $s < 1/2$. Voting as though type five, however, leads to a value of $s - 1$ which is successful for all $s < 1$. Carrying out all computations, we obtain the following list of useful strategies.

(29)

| Type | Strategy | $s$ methods | Strategy | $s$ methods |
|------|----------|-------------|----------|-------------|
| 4 | 5 | $s < 1$ | 6 | $s < \frac{1}{2}$ |
| 5 | None | | | |
| 6 | 5 | $s > 0$ | 4 | $s > \frac{1}{2}$ |

For instance, if Machiavelli has sincere preferences $C \succ B \succ A$ (type 4) and a burning desire for $B$ to beat $A$ with the $(6, 5, 0)$ voting procedure (so, $s = 5/6$), then, according to Eq. 29, his only manipulative strategy is to vote as though his preferences are $B \succ C \succ A$ (type 5). On the other hand, if Machiavelli's sincere preferences were $B \succ C \succ A$ (type 5), then he is powerless; according to Eq. 29 there is no way he can strategically vote to alter the conclusion.

Of course, for a strategy to be effective, either the sincere election outcome must be close to an $A \approx B$ tie, or enough voters must join forces. To determine how a mixed coalition should vote strategically, use the same analysis where the "change vector" $\mathbf{v}$ is a sum of the vectors describing the changes for each voter.

**5.1. Runoffs and other behavior.** Somewhat surprisingly, learning how to politically connive reduces to a mathematics problem of finding certain normal vectors and then taking appropriate scalar products. This description suggests that, in general, the more "tied" surfaces a procedure admits (so there are more normal vectors), the more varied the admissible strategies and opportunities. A procedure with several stages, for instance, admits "tied surfaces" at each stage.

Consider, for instance, a runoff election where after dropping bottom-ranked candidate(s) from a first election, a second (or third, or fourth) election is held. The "tied election" surfaces for the first election determine who will be advanced to the second stage, so the strategies represent trying to advance weaker candidates to help your preferred choice win in the final election. This is a well-used approach. After all, our election for the U.S. President has this staged property with the primaries and a general election. The constant fear is that voters from one party will manipulatively vote in the other party's primary to ensure a weaker, more vulnerable opponent.

This returns us to the Michigan Presidential primary in March 2000, where many independents and voters from the Democratic party crossed party lines to vote for Sen. McCain over Gov. Bush. I would love to claim that this cross-over vote illustrates this manipulative strategy, but it appears that, instead of being strategic, many of these voters really did want McCain. On the other hand, there are many primary elections where it strongly appears that the cross-over vote elected a weaker candidate for the "other" party. Indeed, the approach is sufficiently obvious that several states, such as California, enacted laws to discourage this manipulative behavior; only voters registered as in a particular party can vote in that primary. Quite frankly, this is a reasonable law.

**5.2. Agendas.** An example of this staged behavior is a meeting agenda $\langle A, B, C \rangle$. The first two specified candidates, $A$ and $B$, are compared in a majority vote, and the winner is advanced to a majority vote with $C$ to determine the overall winner. To illustrate with an example, suppose the preferences for nine voters are

| Number | Ranking | Number | Ranking |
|--------|---------|--------|---------|
| 4 | $A \succ B \succ C$ | 4 | $B \succ C \succ A$ |
| 1 | $C \succ A \succ B$ | | |

(30)

where, to add intrigue, suppose your preferences are $A \succ B \succ C$. Your favored candidate $A$ beats $B$ by 5:4 and advances to the final stage against $C$. Unfortunately, the candidate you dread, $C$, wins with a 5:4 vote.

What are your strategies? There are no options at the final stage because your only choices are to vote for $A$ or for despised $C$. But at the first stage, by voting for $B$ instead of your favored $A$, the final election is between $B$ and $C$ where $B$ beats $C$. Although your favorite $A$ does not win, neither does your least favored $C$.

As an aside, the "$\mathbf{v}$" appearing in Eq. 27 models much more than strategic action. It can be used to determine what happens with *any* vote change where, say, voters refuse or forget to vote, new voters join, subcommittees join as a full committee, and so forth. All of these questions can be similarly analyzed: i.e., find the appropriate normals $\mathbf{N}$, determine the change vectors $\mathbf{v}$ for the different behaviors, and compute the scalar product.

To illustrate, suppose you and a friend with the same $A \succ B \succ C$ preferences either forgot to vote, or headed for the beach. Could your negligence be rewarded with a personally better election outcome? It can. In the agenda example, for instance, by not voting, it is $B$ who wins; $B$, instead of $A$, wins the first stage and goes on to beat $C$. Had both of you voted, and voted sincerely, you would have suffered by having $C$ as the winner. Ah, the perversity of voting procedures!

I leave it to the reader to characterize the kinds of procedures which allow such a pathological behavior. (For this inverse problem, note that if type-$j$ voter doesn't vote, $\mathbf{v} = -\mathbf{e}_j$; this is the unit six-dimensional vector with unity in the $j$ component. Next, characterize the appropriate kinds of normal vectors allowing this outcome.) Another challenge is to determine which kinds of procedures can *punish* a candidate should she receive more support (they exist!); namely, the winning candidate loses only because more of her supporters voted.

# Chapter 5

# What *Do* the Voters Want?

So far, we have been deluged with negative news. Even after exploring several different voting stances — changing the weights of the procedure, dropping candidates, combining methods — we have been continually exposed to more and more annoying problems which describe new ways for something to go "wrong." Enough is enough; no more pessimism. It is time to understand what can go "right." To take a first step in this direction, I address the issue, "What do the voters really want?"

There is no unique answer for this question. It is impossible to say what the voters had in mind when casting all of those ballots. Yet, it is possible to make a first cut at addressing this concern. It is interesting that by doing so, we venture beyond suggesting what the voters might want to developing a methodology which characterizes all possible flaws and voting paradoxes that can ever occur with any positional procedure.[1] The approach even allows us to describe all profiles which can cause these difficulties; it allows us to explain what can go right and what can go wrong with any specified profile when used with different voting procedures.

The reader might react to this last comment with a dismayed, "What! More problems?" Actually, a complete story describes a messier, more troubling set of voting situations.[2] However, let's leave these perversities behind

---

[1] Or, methods such as runoff and AV which use these procedures.

[2] For instance, Chapter 2 describes what can happen when different procedures are used with the same set of candidates, and Chapter 3 describes what happens as candidates are dropped or added. The story describing what happens by combining both approaches shows that voting offers even more troublesome results than those already described.

and concentrate on finding positive assertions. The encouraging news is that the measures developed for "what the voters really want" isolate a unique procedure, the Borda Count, which meets all expectations.

## 1. Breaking ties and cycles

The key theme involves "cancellations." After all, "cancellation" is a central notion for validating the meaning of an election tally. For instance, if it were not so difficult to carry out the actual task, a natural way to determine the election outcome after opening the ballot box would be to first match "opposing votes." After gathering all of these votes which cancel each other to create a tied outcome, the tie is broken by the votes which remain. These extra votes determine the winner.

To illustrate with a simple example, suppose in a two-person contest that Maria received 30 votes and Jill receives 20; Maria, of course, wins by 10 votes. To use the cancelling approach, pair each "Maria vote" with a "Jill vote." As Maria and Jill are the only candidates, each pair of opposing votes creates a tied outcome; the 20 pairings defines a "Maria $\approx$ Jill" conclusion. This tie is broken by the remaining ten ballots; as all of them favor Maria, Maria wins "with a surplus of ten votes."

The approach developed here extends this simple notion. The goal is to understand the different collections and arrangements of ballots which should cancel to generate a tie. In this manner, it becomes possible to find a first approximation for "what the voters want."

Even more is possible. By understanding which collection of ballots should define a "tie," we can analyze voting methods. Namely, if a voting method delivers something other than a tied outcome when no candidate should be favored, then this "voting anomaly" identifies a bias, or weakness, of the procedure. In this manner, explanations are found for all of the voting paradoxes described in the earlier chapters.

**1.1. "For a price ... " revisited.** Recall my earlier challenge (page 100) that,

> *For a price, I will come to your organization just prior to your next important election. You tell me who you want to win. I will talk with the voters to determine their preferences over the candidates. Then, I will design a "democratic voting method" which involves all candidates. In the election, the specified candidate will win.*

This challenge, which is intended to dramatically emphasize the critical role played by the choice of an election procedure, usually is not overly difficult to meet. Indeed, the methodology developed next describes how to identify which procedures give different answers for the same profile, so it shows how to meet the challenge. Let me start by explaining how I constructed the profile illustrating the original challenge.

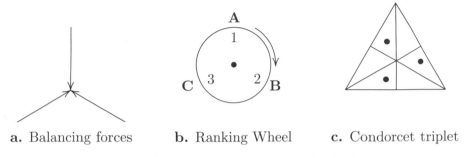

**a.** Balancing forces     **b.** Ranking Wheel     **c.** Condorcet triplet

**Fig. 5.1.** Finding symmetry $(Z_3)$

First, we need to understand what constitutes a "cancellation." Insight comes from Fig. 5.1a which illustrates three balancing forces acting on a point. Think of this as representing three people pushing on a ball, each with equal force in the indicated direction. It is the symmetry, the 120° balancing separation of each person's effort, which cancels their efforts to keep the ball in equilibrium.

To capture a similar "120°" separation in the design of profiles, use what I call a "ranking wheel." As depicted in Fig. 5.1b, mount this freely rotating disk on a wall. Equally spaced along the wheel's edge — that is, at a 120° separation — are the "ranking numbers" 1, 2, and 3. To use this wheel to generate preference rankings, start with any ranking, say $A \succ B \succ C$. Next to each ranking number, mark on the wall the name of the candidate ranked in that position. So, as displayed in Fig. 5.1b, mark $A$ next to "1," $B$ next to "2", and $C$ next to "3."

To create new rankings, rotate the wheel in the indicated clockwise manner until the "1" is by the next name. This new location of the ranking numbers places each candidate in a new position; write down the associated ranking. Continue this process until each candidate has been "top ranked" precisely once. The resulting set of three rankings,

(31) $$A \succ B \succ C, \quad B \succ C \succ A, \quad C \succ A \succ B,$$

is called the *Condorcet triplet*.

It is interesting to notice that when this profile is listed in Fig. 5.1c with our standard geometric approach, the bullets again define a 120° separation within the triangle. Moreover, this construction, which mathematicians call "a $Z_3$ orbit" of the original ranking, defines a profile which, arguably, defines a natural cancellation of opposing views. The argument for the tie is obvious;

according to the construction, no candidate has an advantage as each is ranked in first, second, and third position precisely once.

Indeed, I know of no argument which even hints that the outcome of this profile should be anything other than a complete tie. Consequently, this symmetry captured by the Condorcet profile constitutes an arrangement of preferences which should define an election tie; it should correspond to a "cancellation of ballots."

**1.2. What methods respect this symmetry?** Now that this rotational arrangement of preferences has been identified, it is reasonable to wonder which of the principal voting procedures respect this cancellation of views.

It is encouraging to discover that all $\mathbf{w}_s = (1, s, 0)$ positional methods deliver the expected $A \approx B \approx C$ completely tied conclusion. The reason is easy to see; since each candidate is in first, second, and last place precisely once, each candidate receives the same $1 + s$ tally.

The situation changes drastically with pairwise voting. Indeed, by computing the pairwise outcomes by using the geometric approach with the Fig. 5.1c representation, it follows that rather than the anticipated tie, this profile defines the pairwise voting cycle

$$(32) \qquad\qquad A \succ B, \quad B \succ C, \quad C \succ A$$

where each victory is by a 2:1 tally.

Another way to compute this cyclic outcome is to express each ranking in terms of its pairs. Then, in each column, compute the election outcome.

|  | **Ranking** | $\{A, B\}$ | $\{B, C\}$ | $\{A, C\}$ |
|---|---|---|---|---|
| (33) | $A \succ B \succ C$ | $A \succ B$ | $B \succ C$ | $A \succ C$ |
|  | $B \succ C \succ A$ | $B \succ A$ | $B \succ C$ | $C \succ A$ |
|  | $C \succ A \succ B$ | $A \succ B$ | $C \succ B$ | $C \succ A$ |
|  | **Outcome** | $A \succ B$ | $B \succ C$ | $C \succ A$ |

Intuition about the source of this election oddity — an election cycle — comes from the force diagram of Fig. 5.1a. Start by imagining a student, who tries to analyze what happens by considering only two of the forces while ignoring the third. So, only the effects of two people pushing on the ball are considered while the efforts of the third person are ignored. Because this myopic analysis is incapable of capturing the full symmetry of the force diagram, it leads to the incorrect conclusion that, instead of the ball being in equilibrium, it is moving — the student thinks the ball should be moving in a direction opposite to the ignored force.

A remarkably similar story explains the pairwise voting cycle. As a computation using Fig. 5.1c displays, the pairwise vote is not capable of recognizing the full symmetry of the Condorcet profile.[3] Instead, by concentrating on what happens to two particular candidates while ignoring the placement of the third, the pairwise outcome erroneously suggests an election movement which favors one candidate over the other.

It is interesting to notice that even though the pairwise vote fails to capture the cancelling effects of the profile, the profile's symmetry still manages to be manifested — by the pairwise cyclic outcomes. This "symmetry breaking" effect is a general mathematical phenomenon. In the force diagram, for instance, while the "two-force" analysis breaks the inherent symmetry, the three "partial solutions" create a symmetric distribution.

As a parting comment before exploring electoral consequences of this loss of symmetry, notice that it is possible to combine the partial information to recover the actual equilibrium setting. For instance, by adding the three force diagram partial answers — the descriptions of movement when considering only two forces — the sum of these motions cancel to reflect the actual situation. Similarly, by adding the pairwise tallies — that is, adding $A$'s tally from both of her two pairwise votes, etc. — the outcome returns to the natural tied conclusion. It turns out that this addition of pairwise tallies always agrees with the Borda Count tally of the profile.

**1.3. Consequences.** To handle more candidates, just place the appropriate number of ranking numbers on a ranking wheel. Then, by specifying a starting ranking for the candidates, construct a Condorcet profile in the above manner. Figure 5.2, for instance, depicts the construction of an eight-candidate Condorcet profile. Since each candidate is to be top ranked precisely once, an eight-candidate example generates a profile with eight preference rankings.

Again, because this construction ranks each candidate in each position precisely once, it follows that all positional methods recognize the cancellation of ballots and deliver a complete tie. Similarly, as the pairwise tally of a Condorcet profile cannot recognize the full symmetry, with any number of candidates, the pairwise outcomes always define a cycle.

---

[3] As just one of many reasons why the pairwise vote fails, its natural symmetries are reflected by $Z_2$; e.g., either a pairwise ranking remains the same or it is reversed. But the $Z_3$ symmetry of the Condorcet profile does not have a subgroup of order two.

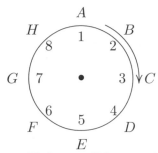

**Figure 5.2.** Eight-candidate ranking wheel

Laborious computations are not needed; the cycle can be read off of the starting ranking. For instance, as the Fig. 5.2 original ranking is $A \succ B \succ C \succ D \succ E \succ F \succ G \succ H$, the pairwise rankings of this profile has each candidate preferred to the following candidate. So, the cycle is

$$A \succ B, \quad B \succ C, \dots, G \succ H, \quad H \succ A.$$

Moreover, the election tallies in this cycle depend on the number of candidates; with $N$ candidates, the tallies are by the overwhelming vote of $(N - 1) : 1$. This is captured by the $N = 3$ candidate example of Fig. 5.1b where all tallies are 2:1; in the $N = 8$ candidate example of Fig. 5.2, all tallies are 7:1.[4]

This rotating effect is so strong that even small portions of the "ranking wheel" construction can foment unusual pairwise behavior. To illustrate with Fig. 5.2, instead of creating a full Condorcet profile of eight rankings, move the wheel only three times to create the set of rankings

$$A \succ B \succ C \succ D \succ E \succ F \succ G \succ H,$$
$$B \succ C \succ D \succ E \succ F \succ G \succ H \succ A,$$
$$C \succ D \succ E \succ F \succ G \succ H \succ A \succ B.$$

Again, this profile's pairwise rankings form a cycle.[5] To make the profile more impressive, instead of assigning just one candidate to each ranking, specify that there are ten of them.

This profile should look familiar; it is the Eq. 25 example used in the original "For a price!" challenge on page 100. When a profile allows cyclic pairwise outcomes, it is easy to create a voting approach to elect "your"

---

[4]More generally, if candidates are $s$ candidates apart in the original ranking, then the tally is $(N - s) : s$. For instance, in Fig. 5.2, $C$ is $s = 2$ candidates away from $A$, so the $A \succ C$ pairwise tally is $(8 - 2) : 2$. $F$ is $s = 5$ candidates away, so the $\{A, F\}$ tally is $(8 - 5) : 5$ meaning an $F \succ A$ ranking.

[5]This approach of creating a cycle by using only the first three "ranking wheel" rankings holds for any number of candidates.

candidate. Just exploit the cycle by listing, and then comparing, the candidates in a reversed order where the "designated winner" is considered at the end of the process. This is, of course, the Fig. 4.3 agenda construction.

We should wonder whether this "ranking wheel" argument explains other puzzles. Does it address all of those concerns raised by the large literature illustrating various unexpected conclusions coming from pairwise comparisons? It does; examples illustrating all of these consequences and unexpected outcomes can be constructed by using the ranking wheel. For instance, all examples of seedings for basketball tournaments, where it is arguable that a "weak" team won, must involve terms from a ranking wheel construction.

In fact, it is a consequence of Thm. 10 given next that *for any method using pairwise rankings or tallies, for all examples indicating problems with the choice of an agenda, or unexpected outcomes from tournaments, or conflicting conclusions from any method based on pairwise comparisons, or any difficulty or problems of these approaches, or any surprising outcomes of voting results where pairwise conclusions appear to be questionable, etc. — they are strictly due to this "ranking wheel" Condorcet effect!*

To more fully capture this disrupting Condorcet behavior, let $\tau(\{A,B\};\mathbf{p})$ represent the difference between $A$'s and $B$'s pairwise tallies for profile $\mathbf{p}$. To illustrate this notation with the nine-voter profile $\mathbf{p}$ where

- four voters prefer $A \succ B \succ D \succ C$,
- three prefer $D \succ B \succ A \succ C$, and
- two prefer $C \succ A \succ D \succ B$,

we have that $\tau(\{A,B\},\mathbf{p}) = (4+2)-3 = 3$, that $\tau(\{B,A\},\mathbf{p}) = 3-(4+2) = -3$, and that $\tau(\{C,D\},\mathbf{p}) = 2 - (4+3) = -5$. This $\tau$ function, then, just measures the "distance" between the two tallies.

This "distance" analogy suffers. To explain, on a line, the distance between points $\mathbf{a}$ and $\mathbf{b}$ plus the distance between $\mathbf{b}$ and $\mathbf{c}$ always equals the distance between $\mathbf{a}$ and $\mathbf{c}$. But pairwise rankings need not be transitive, so it is highly unlikely for this nice additive relationship to hold with their tallies. Indeed, with our simple example, because $\tau(\{A,B\},\mathbf{p}) = 3$, $\tau(\{B,C\},\mathbf{p}) = 5$, and $\tau(\{A,C\},\mathbf{p}) = 5$, we do not have the desired $\tau(\{A,B\},\mathbf{p}) + \tau(\{B,C\},\mathbf{p}) = \tau(\{A,C\},\mathbf{p})$.

Nevertheless, this condition, which goes far beyond transitivity to require the tallies to be well behaved, deserves a name.

**Definition 2** (Saari [**56**])**.** If for all triplets of candidates $\{A,B,C\}$ a profile $\mathbf{p}$ has the property that

$$(34) \qquad \tau(\{A,B\},\mathbf{p}) + \tau(\{B,C\},\mathbf{p}) = \tau(\{A,C\},\mathbf{p}),$$

then the profile is said to satisfy (pairwise) "additive transitivity."

But why can profiles fail to be additively transitive? As with everything else, when something goes wrong with pairwise voting it is safe to blame the Condorcet terms.

**Theorem 10** (Saari [**56**]). *For any number of candidates, all pairwise voting cycles and all paradoxes involving pairwise voting outcomes are due to components of the Condorcet profiles.*

*Indeed, for a given profile* **p**, *suppose all components in the Condorcet directions are removed. Represent the "Condorcet-free" portion of the profile by* **p**\*. *Not only are the pairwise rankings of* **p**\* *always transitive, but differences in tallies always satisfy additive transitivity; that is, they mimic the additive properties of distances between points on a line.*[6]

The additive transitivity assertion is a major surprise; it dramatically demonstrates that all possible problems with pairwise voting are completely due to the Condorcet terms. Not only are the Condorcet terms totally responsible for all violations of transitive rankings and associated oddities — such as cycles, settings where the choice of an agenda can alter the conclusion, problems with tournaments, settings where the societal pairwise rankings may differ from those obtained by other procedures, and so forth — but these Condorcet terms even keep differences between the tallies from adding in a natural manner. In other words, the "Condorcet terms" generate a form of "noise" which disrupts the intent of the voters. Later in this chapter I describe how to eliminate these troubling components.

**1.4. More consequences.** France, in the 1780s, was a busy time for Condorcet. In addition to his contributions to the changing spirit and attitudes which fueled the French Revolution, he was among the leaders who believed that, similar to the physical world, human society is subject to natural laws.

Beyond his discussions with Benjamin Franklin and the many intellectuals passing through Paris, including his close friend the American minister to the French court Thomas Jefferson, about the exciting notions being exported to the world by the American Revolution,[7] Condorcet made early contributions to theory of probability and he pioneered the application of mathematical methods to political problems. "Condorcet believed passionately in reason, and reason to him meant mathematics. ... He embraced the Revolution with enthusiasm, for it promised to usher in the ... final

---

[6]The "removal" of Condorcet components uses a vector analysis approach. This is explained in Saari [**54**] where a geometric approach also is described which characterizes all possible pairwise outcomes that can occur over three alternatives. In this space, the outcomes for the additive transitive profiles define what I call a "transitivity plane."

[7]See, for instance, Adams' book [**1**] "The Paris Years of Thomas Jefferson."

epoch, in which human society would reach its perfections — supervised, of course, by mathematicians and statisticians."[8] But rather than witnessing a philosopher using an integral sign for a scepter, the turn of political events with the slide into the Reign of Terror cost Condorcet his life.

A natural portion of Condorcet's agenda involved the study of voting procedures. Earlier, his colleague in the Academy of Sciences, J. C. de Borda, introduced his voting procedure now called the Borda Count. Condorcet strongly disagreed with Borda's philosophy, and, quite frankly, he really did not have much respect for Borda. Rather than using a positional method, such as the Borda Count, Condorcet embraced "head-to-head" comparisons; he believed in the pairwise vote.

His arguments were so persuasive that even today the "Condorcet winner" is the widely accepted standard for voting procedures. This means that a serious blemish on the character of a procedure is if it fails to always elect the Condorcet winner. This attitude is amply reflected by the contemporary literature with its several articles exploring the "Condorcet principle."

As a means to demonstrate the potential dangers of using positional methods — perhaps to discredit the Borda Count — Condorcet designed the Fig. 5.3a profile. By using the geometric approach to tally the ballots, it follows that the $\mathbf{w}_s$ positional rankings are $B \succ A \succ C$ with the tally $39+31s : 31+39s : 11+11s$. Condorcet's point is that this common positional outcome fails to elect the Condorcet winner $A$. As demonstrated in Fig. 5.3a, $A$ beats both $B$ and $C$ in pairwise comparisons.

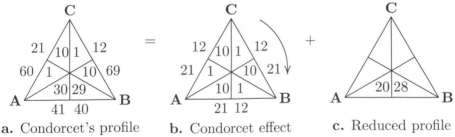

**a.** Condorcet's profile      **b.** Condorcet effect      **c.** Reduced profile

**Fig. 5.3.** A historically important profile

There is no question that Condorcet's example has had a tremendous impact on the field. Even though very few professionals in this research area know the Fig. 5.3a profile, they know that it exists, and they often invoke this fact as a criticism of the Borda Count. After all, since the BC is a positional method, this profile proves that the Borda Count need not elect the Condorcet winner.

But does Condorcet's example illustrate a weakness of the positional methods, or does it locate the Achilles' heel of his approach? Namely, does

---

[8]Herold, [**24**] page 91.

this example expose a subtle but serious flaw of the "Condorcet winner"? Remember, the votes from the Condorcet portion of a profile — the portion that is constructed by using the ranking wheel — should cancel to create a tie. This suggests analyzing the example by separating the Condorcet portion — which should end in a tie — from what is left.

The decomposition is natural; just subtract as large of a fixed number as possible from each of the two 120° pinwheel configurations. For instance, the configuration with the $A \succ C \succ B$ ranking consists of the values $1, 1, 29$, so the largest number that can be subtracted from each of them is "1." Similarly, the other "pinwheel" allows "10's" to be subtracted from each of the three entries. These values, the two Condorcet portions, are illustrated in Fig. 5.3b; the portion which remains after the subtraction — the portion that should "break the tie" with the cancellation story — is in Fig. 5.3c.

The appropriate societal outcome to assign to the remaining Fig. 5.3c profile is obvious. The disregard these voters have for $C$, by unanimously ranking her at the bottom, converts this election into a de facto two-candidate race where $B$ enjoys a eight-vote edge over $A$. Indeed, this natural $B \succ A \succ C$ outcome is supported by the pairwise vote and almost all other voting procedures.[9]

Now consider the effects of the Condorcet portion depicted in Fig. 5.3b. Adding this term — which should cancel and which has no effect on positional rankings — to the Fig. 5.3c profile radically twists the pairwise tallies in the indicated cyclic manner. It is this clockwise twist which crowns $A$, rather than $B$, as the Condorcet winner. In other words, this portion of the profile which should lead to a cancellation of votes is what determines the Condorcet winner.

So, rather than supporting Condorcet's intent, it is arguable that his example illustrates a serious weakness of the Condorcet winner. The inability of the pairwise vote to recognize the "ranking wheel" symmetry forces the procedure to count votes that should have canceled. Rather than measuring the voters' intent, it is very possible that the usual standard, the Condorcet winner, reflects a "twist" in the tallies caused by a mistaken interpretation of a certain collection of votes.

**1.5. Constructing examples.** While Fig. 5.3 indicates how to extract the Condorcet portion out of a profile to explain unexpected behavior, it also shows how to create as many new "paradoxes" as desired. The approach, which is illustrated below, is simple. Instead of starting from the left and moving to the right in Fig. 5.3, start at the right, at Fig. 5.3c, and work to the left.

---

[9]The antiplurality ranking differs; it is $A \approx B \succ C$.

To illustrate with a motivating goal, notice that Condorcet' Fig. 5.3a profile does not quite do as advertised. This is because the antiplurality ranking of the Fig. 5.3a and 5.3c profiles allow a $A \approx B \succ C$ ranking where the Condorcet winner is tied for the top place. So, as a first challenge, I create an example where *all positional methods strictly rank the Condorcet winner in second place.*

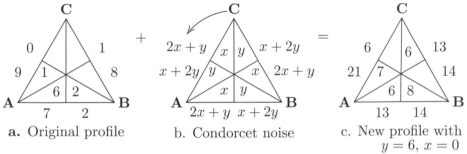

**a.** Original profile    b. Condorcet noise    c. New profile with $y = 6,\ x = 0$

**Fig. 5.4** Creating examples

Start with a profile where the positional outcomes have a desired behavior. For instance, the Fig. 5.4a example has six voters preferring Andrea $\succ$ Bobbie $\succ$ Candy; one voter differs only between whether Bobbie or Candy should be bottom ranked, while only two voters rank Bobbie above Andrea. All $\mathbf{w}_s = (1, s, 0)$ tallies $(7+2s : 2+6s : s)$ of this profile support the natural outcome of Andrea $\succ$ Bobbie $\succ$ Candy. Even the pairwise rankings agree with this common conclusion.

To create conflict, add an undetermined number of voters whose votes should "cancel" — a Condorcet portion. Select these preferences so that they "twist" the pairwise tallies in a desired direction. In Fig. 5.4b, the two choices of Condorcet terms are indicated by the unknowns $x$ and $y$; the choice of these values depends on what we want from the constructed profile.

For a first example, let's create a profile to meet Condorcet's goals; namely, create an example where all positional methods have the Andrea $\succ$ Bobbie $\succ$ Candy ranking, but Bobbie is the Condorcet winner.

This is easy to do. The arrow in Fig. 5.4b shows the cycling direction which adds more to Bobbie's pairwise vote than to Andrea's. Since the $x$ value moves the cycle in the wrong direction, set $x = 0$ and solve for the $y$ value which offers the correct level of cyclic assistance. Namely, for Bobbie to beat Andrea, solve the inequality

$$2 + 2y > 7 + y, \quad \text{or } y > 5.$$

For Bobbie to also beat Candy, we need

$$8 + y > 1 + 2y, \quad \text{or } y < 7.$$

Combining the two inequalities, the $y = 6$ choice changes the pairwise outcomes so that, rather than Andrea, Bobbie now is the Condorcet winner; this profile with $y = 6$ is represented in Fig. 5.4c. Again, because the Condorcet terms do not affect the rankings of positional methods, the positional ranking determined by the Fig. 5.4a component persists.

The same approach can be used to create profiles exhibiting whatever is desired — as long as the example is possible. For instance, how about keeping the same positional rankings, but creating a situation where Candy beats Andrea. No problem. Such an example requires the pairwise tallies to cycle in a clockwise direction. As the $y$ values move the tallies in a conflicting direction, set $y = 0$ and solve the inequality

$$0 + 2x > 9 + x.$$

Any $x > 9$ will suffice.

But a $x > 9$ value generates such a heavy clockwise spin that it forces the final pairwise tallies to cycle; the societal outcomes are $C \succ A$, $A \succ B$, $B \succ C$. The reason why it is impossible to start with the Fig. 5.4a profile and make $C$ the Condorcet winner follows from algebra; if $C$ is to also beat $B$, then $x$ must satisfy $1 + x > 8 + 2x$, or $-7 > x$. Clearly, the $-7 > x$ and $x > 9$ conditions are seriously incompatible. (Even if $y$ is included, there are no solutions.)

A related explanation uses the fact that the Condorcet term does not affect the positional rankings; as such, the Borda Count ranking is determined solely by the Fig. 5.4a portion of the final profile. Earlier I stated the new ([**54**, **56**]) assertion that, with transitive pairwise rankings, the Borda winner, Andrea, cannot be pairwise ranked below the Borda loser, Candy. As Candy beats Andrea, the pairwise rankings cannot be transitive.

**1.6. Losing rationality.** What is going on? A way to extract a deeper explanation for this cyclic phenomenon uses Table 33; for convenience, this table is reproduced next.

| Ranking | $\{A, B\}$ | $\{B, C\}$ | $\{A, C\}$ |
|---|---|---|---|
| $A \succ B \succ C$ | $A \succ B$ | $B \succ C$ | $A \succ C$ |
| $B \succ C \succ A$ | $B \succ A$ | $B \succ C$ | $C \succ A$ |
| $C \succ A \succ B$ | $A \succ B$ | $C \succ B$ | $C \succ A$ |
| **Outcome** | $A \succ B$ | $B \succ C$ | $C \succ A$ |

Remember, the pairwise vote is merely an algorithm; it just counts the number of voters who prefer each candidate. In particular, the procedure has no way to determine who voted in what manner in each of the three elections. Consequently, the pairwise vote provides identical tallies and rankings for any listing of preferences with the same number of voters preferring $A$ to $B$, etc.

A way to find all of these associated profiles is to mix and match the pairwise rankings that are listed in the table.[10] This defines the following *five different profiles.*

1. The Condorcet profile. Here, it is arguable that the outcome should be a tie. It is not; it is a cycle.

2. The profile where two voters have the *cyclic* preferences $A \succ B$, $B \succ C$, $C \succ A$, while the last voter has the reversed cyclic preferences $A \succ C$, $C \succ B$, $B \succ A$. The only difference between the voters is whether the cycle should go one way or the other, so the cyclic outcome is a natural conclusion as this direction is supported by 2:1.

3. The last three profiles have one voter with a transitive ranking, say $A \succ B \succ C$, while the other voter has the opposite transitive ranking; here it would be $C \succ B \succ A$. These directly opposing preferences cancel to cause a tie. The tie is broken by the remaining voter's preferences — the cyclic $A \succ C$, $C \succ B$, $B \succ A$. Again, the cyclic outcome is a natural conclusion for these profiles.

The pairwise vote finds these five different profiles to be indistinguishable. For four of them, the cycle is a perfectly reasonable societal outcome. Only for the Condorcet choice — the only profile consisting of transitive preferences — is the outcome questionable. This example, which identifies all the unintended cyclic profiles, suggests that contrary to our intentions, the pairwise vote is trying to meet the needs of nonexistent cyclic voters. (This interpretation is made precise, and implications developed in Saari and Sieberg [63] and in Saari [60].)

To summarize what we have learned about the Condorcet portion,

1. It is arguable that the Condorcet profile, which comes from the ranking wheel construction, identifies a collection of ballots which should cancel and result in a tie vote.

2. Because the pairwise voting procedure cannot recognize the full symmetry of the Condorcet profile, the pairwise outcome is a cycle.

3. The pairwise cycle occurs because the pairwise vote cannot distinguish whether the Condorcet portion of a profile involves the intended transitive voters (called "rationality" in the literature) or voters with cyclic preferences.

---

[10] In other words, pairwise tallies define mappings over the domain of binary rankings. The "mix-and-match" approach to find all associated profiles determines the inverse image of the cyclic outcomes. My main point is that the transitive rankings form only a small section of this inverse image.

4. An immediate consequence is that *any procedure based on the pairwise vote, including the "Condorcet winner," runs the risk that its conclusion is seriously biased by views of nonexistent cyclic voters.*

No wonder the methods which are based on pairwise voting can cause so much trouble.

**1.7. Return to Arrow's Theorem.** Incidentally, this observation about the effects of the Condorcet portion of a profile explains Arrow's Theorem. While a more complete and detailed discussion of Arrow's result along with several related issues is described in my book (Saari [**60**]), let me offer a brief glimpse into this new interpretation of Arrow's Theorem. I do so, in part, because mathematicians, economists, political scientists and others are quoted in the press using Arrow's Theorem as a means to explain away the 2000 election. Typical quotes, which claim that "Arrow's Theorem proves that no method is fair," or, "There's a mathematical result known as Arrow's theorem which says very roughly that there is never a fool-proof way to derive group preferences from individual preferences that can be absolutely guaranteed [**37**]," leave a sense of futility. But is this what the theorem really means?

To start, since we have no intentions of embracing a dictatorship, Arrow's Theorem (see the material starting on page 28) concludes that no procedure can satisfy some seemingly innocuous conditions. Among his requirements, Arrow mandates that the voters have transitive preferences and he considers only procedures which satisfy "Independence of Irrelevant Alternatives" (IIA). Remember, when the procedure is determining the societal ranking of two alternatives, IIA restricts the procedure to use only the information about these alternatives — nothing else. For instance, "pairwise voting" satisfies IIA; when computing the pairwise ranking of $\{A, B\}$, information about all other alternatives is irrelevant.

To identify the source of Arrow's Theorem, suppose when Lillian considers the three basketball teams {Lakers, Bulls, Knicks}, she prefers the Lakers to the Bulls. Are her preferences transitive over these three choices? It is, of course, impossible to answer this question without more information. After all, "transitivity of preferences" is a sequencing condition; it checks whether the pairwise rankings of the three pairs fit a particular pattern.

Now notice that IIA *prohibits* the procedure from using any information needed to validate the transitivity of the voters. Just as with the limited information provided about Lillian's choices, by insisting on using only pairwise data, IIA dismisses all information needed to determine whether a voter has, or does not have, transitive preferences. The "transitivity of preferences," in other words, plays absolutely no role in determining the societal outcomes. Instead, as with pairwise voting and a sufficiently heterogeneous profile, the procedure tries to service nonexistent cyclic voters.

A way to underscore this point is to recall that the "cyclic voter misinterpretation" is caused by the Condorcet portion of a profile. This suggests that if my argument is correct, then positive assertions should follow by eliminating the Condorcet effects from the profile. This happens.

**Theorem 11** (Saari [**56, 60**]). *For any number of candidates, suppose the Condorcet component is removed from all profiles. The assumptions of Arrow's Theorem are satisfied by the Borda Count.*

So, rather than the traditional "no method is fair" claims, Arrow's Theorem means that procedures which consider separately how voters treat each pair lose valuable information — they lose the assumption that the voters have transitive preferences. This claim is further supported by the following assertion.

**Theorem 12** (Saari [**56, 60**]). *Suppose Arrow's IIA condition is modified so that the procedure depends not only on how each voter ranks each pair of candidates, but also on information which verifies that the voters have transitive preferences — in particular, it also uses the number of candidates a voter ranks between the two specified candidates. The Borda Count satisfies this modified form of IIA and Arrow's other conditions. No other positional method satisfies these conditions.*

In our quest for a procedure which avoids the previously described nightmares which can plague election procedures, only the Borda Count has surfaced. The BC plays a particularly central role for avoiding problems identified with pairwise comparisons and Arrow's Theorem. Since the Borda Count is the main successful voting method at this stage, it is wise to keep track of how it fares with the next set of "cancelling ballots."

## 2. Reversal effects

Fred and his wife Julia share common interests in sports, restaurants, and cultural events. But, well, even though they love each other, they almost always have precisely opposing political opinions. For instance, in the forthcoming election, Fred prefers $A \succ B \succ C$ while Julia prefers $C \succ B \succ A$.

On the other hand, this conflict can work to their advantage. This is because the election conflicts with their deep desire to see a great basketball game between the two teams tied for the conference lead. After much discussion, Fred and Julia agree that because their directly opposing political views only cancel, with a clear conscience they can skip their voting duties to travel to the basketball game.

**2.1. Voting methods.** This brief story identifies another symmetry setting, one the mathematicians would call a "$Z_2$ orbit," where the collection of opposing preferences should cancel. But do all voting procedures respect this reversal symmetry?

The pairwise vote most surely respects this reversal effect. We can see this with Fred's and Julia's opposing views. The ranking of each pair, say $\{A, C\}$, in Fred's $A \succ B \succ C$ preferences is the direct opposite of Julia's ranking of this pair. As this is true for all pairs, all pairwise tallies from their two votes cancel to create a tie.

On the other hand, rather than the soothing tie, conflicting election results occur with the $\mathbf{w}_s$ positional procedures. The $\mathbf{w}_s$ tally would be

(35)

|  | $A$ | $B$ | $C$ |
|---|---|---|---|
| Fred's vote | 1 | $s$ | 0 |
| Julia's vote | 0 | $s$ | 1 |
| **Total** | 1 | $2s$ | 1 |

As the tally shows, $A$ and $C$ each receive one point while $B$ receives $2s$ points. Thus, the different $\mathbf{w}_s$ rankings for this profile follow:

| $\mathbf{w}_s$ **procedures** | **Election Ranking** |
|---|---|
| $s < \frac{1}{2}$ | $A \approx C \succ B$ |
| $s = \frac{1}{2}$ | $A \approx B \approx C$ |
| $s > \frac{1}{2}$ | $B \succ A \approx C.$ |

Only for the Borda Count ($s = \frac{1}{2}$) is the outcome the desired $A \approx B \approx C$ tie. Other than the Borda Count, all other positional methods ignore the reversal symmetry. But, by breaking a symmetry, we should observe related reversal outcomes on each side of the Borda Count. This happens; I leave it to the reader to discover a relationship between distance $|s - \frac{1}{2}|$ and the Eq. 35 tallies causing reversed rankings.

The surprising conclusion (Saari [**54**]) is that, for three candidates, *this reversal symmetry — a collection of rankings which should create a tied vote setting — totally explains all differences between positional tallies.* As a way to illustrate this assertion, let me show how these reversal terms are totally responsible for all of those conflicting election outcomes which arise from the Eq. 8 profile. This profile, which was one of the first illustrations used in this book, is geometrically represented in Fig. 5.5a.

As with the analysis of the Condorcet term, a way to understand this profile is to separate all reversal terms from the original profile to discover what is left. Since the reversal terms (in Fig. 5.5b) should cancel to create a tie, the remaining portion of the profile, which is in Fig. 5.5c, should determine the election outcome.

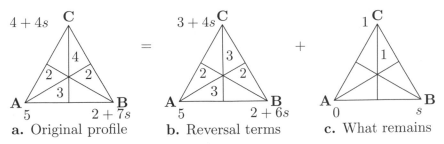

**a.** Original profile      **b.** Reversal terms      **c.** What remains

**Fig. 5.5.** Explaining the Eq. 8 profile

**2.2. A reversal decomposition.** To extract the reversal terms from Fig. 5.5a, notice that opposing rankings are represented by a pair of ranking regions which are on opposite sides of the indifference point. So, subtract the largest possible common value from each pair of opposing ranking regions in Fig. 5.5a. For instance, as the entry in the $A \succ B \succ C$ ranking region of Fig. 5.5a is 3 while the value in the opposite region is 4, subtract 3 from each term. Carrying out this process, the reversal terms are described in Fig. 5.5b; the remaining portion of the profile — the tie breaker — is given in Fig. 5.5c.

This decomposition separates the Fig. 5.5a profile into a set of ten voters and a set of a single voter. The preferences of the ten voters can be paired in a manner which should create a tie. Thus, the $C \succ B \succ A$ preference of the single remaining voter should break this tie.

This "tie-breaker" effect precisely describes what happens with the Borda Count and the pairwise vote; their rankings are not influenced by the reversal terms. The rankings of all other positional methods, however, are strongly affected by the reversal term. Stated in another manner, the reversal portion of the profile is another noisy trouble maker; it is the profile portion which creates all of the bothersome and highly varied positional election rankings. In fact it is the strong reversal component which generates seven different positional rankings for the Fig. 5.5a profile. The paradoxes reflect the different ways procedures treat votes that should cancel.

Of course, instead of viewing Fig. 5.5 in the usual "left-to-right" manner describing the profile decomposition, viewing the figure in a "right-to-left" fashion shows how to start with a simple profile, Fig. 5.5c, and then add an appropriate reversal term, Fig. 5.5b, to create a profile with a desired positional behavior. This approach is illustrated with the use of Fig. 5.6.

Before designing new examples, let me summarize some of what we have discovered.

1. The reversal term has no effect whatsoever on the Borda rankings, but it does cause the tallies of all other positional procedures to differ from

the Borda tally. Thus a base point of the *procedure line* (introduced in Chapter 2, page 46) is the Borda Count normalized tally; the reversal portion of a profile defines the rest of the line.

2. Since a profile's reversal component changes the positional tallies without affecting the pairwise rankings, and the Condorcet portion has no impact on the positional rankings but changes the pairwise tallies, these two "profile noise" effects have an orthogonal nature. Consequently, when creating examples, these two effects can be used separately from each other.

3. We started by identifying collections of ballots which should define a tie vote. Only the Borda Count respects both of these arrangements and delivers the intended tie. In other words, *the Borda Count is the only procedure which is immune to the effects of the Condorcet and the reversal terms.*

**2.3.  Designing examples with reversal terms.** According to the above, to create examples, start with a base profile, add an appropriate Condorcet term to alter the pairwise ranking in a desired manner, and then add a reversal term which alters the positional rankings as planned. To illustrate this construction, I use the Fig. 5.4a base profile. Earlier in Fig. 5.4, I added a Condorcet term to make $B$, rather than $A$, the Condorcet winner. I now show how to design a reversal term so that after choosing a ranking for any $\mathbf{w}_s$ method (other than the Borda Count), a supporting profile can be constructed. To demonstrate, let me design a reversal term which has a $C \succ A \succ B$ plurality ranking.

As before, start with the base profile from Fig. 5.6a and 5.4a. The $u$ and $v$ values of Fig. 5.6b indicate two possible reversal components. By adding the plurality values for Figs. 5.6a and b, it follows that to have a plurality $C \succ A \succ B$ outcome, $u$ and $v$ must be selected to satisfy

(36)                       $$0 + (u + v) > 7 + u > 2 + v.$$

As the first inequality requires $v > 7$, let $v = 8$. With this $v = 8$ value, the second inequality becomes $7 + u > 10$, or $u > 3$. Thus, let $u = 4$. When these values are substituted into Fig. 5.6b and either added to Fig. 5.4c, or added to Fig. 5.6a and Fig. 5.4b, the resulting profile is Fig. 5.6c.

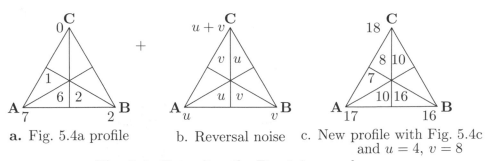

**a.** Fig. 5.4a profile          b. Reversal noise     c. New profile with Fig. 5.4c
                                                        and $u = 4$, $v = 8$

**Fig. 5.6.** Extending the Fig. 5.4 example

For profile Fig. 5.6c,

- the Borda Count outcome is $A \succ B \succ C$ as determined by the starting Fig. 5.6a profile,

- the pairwise ranking, which is designed to have a different Condorcet winner, is $B \succ A \succ C$ — it is determined by the Condorcet portion as given in Fig. 5.4b, and

- the plurality ranking, which is selected to ensure that the remaining candidate $C$ also is a "winner," is $C \succ A \succ B$— it is determined by the reversal components Fig. 5.6b.

In this manner, by varying the choice of the base profile, the Condorcet and reversal components, profiles illustrating all possible three-candidate voting paradoxes can be created.

**2.4. Any number of candidates.** For any number of candidates, the message remains the same. *Only the Borda Count observes all natural collections of ballots which should define a tie.* Namely, all conflicting outcomes from all other methods are based on portions of the profile which should be considered as noise; they distort the outcome by favoring some candidates even though the ballots should cancel.

Of course, by adding candidates, the geometric description of voting jumps into higher-dimensional spaces. In turn, higher-dimensional spaces unleash new kinds of symmetries — symmetries which characterize arrangements of ballots that should constitute tied settings. For any number of candidates, all voting paradoxes, all disagreements among voting methods, all conflicts concerning changes in election rankings when candidates are added or dropped, are consequences of these symmetries.

But, something is missing. To explain, it is not difficult to construct profiles creating a questionable Borda outcome. For instance, every so often

I receive an email or letter asking me to explain the problem with the profile

| | Number | Ranking | Number | Ranking |
|---|---|---|---|---|
| (37) | 3 | $C \succ B \succ A \succ X$ | 2 | $A \succ X \succ C \succ B$ |
| | 2 | $B \succ A \succ X \succ C$ | | |

When only the three candidates $\{A, B, C\}$ are considered, the Borda outcome is $C \succ B \succ A$. This ranking seriously conflicts with the Borda $A \succ B \succ C \succ X$ outcome for all four candidates. As one correspondent wrote,[11] "$X$ is no better than 2nd choice for any voter. [But] the addition of $X$ reverses the rankings of $A$ and $C$ — the last place loser and first place winner in the first [three candidate] case. ... I'm just curious as to whether there is a way around this paradox." To be blunt, he wanted to understand why the Borda Count allowed the weak candidate $X$ to emasculate the fortunes of the strong candidate $C$.

The value of my explanation is that it illustrates *the source of all possible election difficulties with the Borda Count.* To start, is $X$ truly a "weak candidate" while $C$ is a "strong one"? After all, it turns out that these voters prefer $X$ to $C$. Indeed, in pairwise votes, $C$ beats $B$, $B$ beats $A$, $A$ beats $X$, and $X$ beats $C$. This cycle already identifies a potential source of the problem; cycles require a Condorcet component.

To investigate this line of thought, notice that the four-candidate ranking wheel with the starting ranking of $C \succ B \succ A \succ X$ generates the Condorcet four-tuple

$$C \succ B \succ A \succ X, \qquad B \succ A \succ X \succ C,$$
$$A \succ X \succ C \succ B, \qquad X \succ C \succ B \succ A.$$

Again, as no candidate is favored with this profile, since each is in first, second, third, and fourth place precisely once, all positional rankings end in a complete tie $A \approx B \approx C \approx X$.

Now, should candidate $X$ drop out, we are left with the Condorcet triplet $C \succ B \succ A$, $B \succ A \succ C$, and $A \succ C \succ B$ *along* with an extra ranking $C \succ B \succ A$. All positional rankings treat the Condorcet triplet as defining a tie, so the tie is broken by the remaining $C \succ B \succ A$ ranking. In other words, the ranking wheel construction plagues all positional methods including the Borda Count. This dropping of $X$ and ending up with a $C \succ B \succ A$ ranking — the same ranking reversal described in the above example — comes close to explaining the Eq. 37 profile.

This problem mimics what happens with pairwise rankings. Namely, any procedure which ranks only three out of the four candidates cannot observe the full "ranking wheel" symmetric construction. Again, by disturbing a symmetry, expect a "symmetry breaking" effect. This happens; dropping a

---

[11]G. Lipow, 10/4/2000.

candidate from this Condorcet four-tuple leaves a Condorcet triplet and the extra indicated ranking; these extra rankings define a "cycle."

(38)

| Dropped | Extra Ranking | Dropped | Extra Ranking |
|:---:|:---:|:---:|:---:|
| $X$ | $C \succ B \succ A$ | $C$ | $B \succ A \succ X$ |
| $B$ | $A \succ X \succ C$ | $A$ | $X \succ C \succ B$ |

Just as the cyclic pairwise rankings for a Condorcet four-tuple can be read from the starting $C \succ B \succ A \succ X$ by writing down successive pairs — $C \succ B$, $B \succ A$, $A \succ X$, $X \succ C$, the cycle of associated triplets are similarly read from the original ranking to create $C \succ B \succ A$, $B \succ A \succ X$, $A \succ X \succ C$, $X \succ C \succ B$. These extra rankings, of course, generate a cyclic effect among the positional rankings.

*This Condorcet effect is the only term which can affect Borda rankings; it is the source of all possible Borda paradoxes* (Saari [**56, 57**]). All other positional procedures are affected both by the Condorcet behavior and by ignoring other kinds of symmetry. Stated in other words, since the only way the Borda Count runs into inconsistencies and difficulties is by dropping candidates, the more accurate reflection of voter preferences is given by the Borda ranking of all candidates.

So, to create a profile with conflicting Borda outcomes, we must use the Condorcet four-tuple. As the cyclic Condorcet influence requires only three of the rankings, drop the ranking where $X$ is top ranked. Next, assign two voters to each of the remaining three rankings and then add one more $C \succ B \succ A \succ X$ voter. By construction, this Eq. 37 profile is dominated by the ranking wheel effect. As such, the four-candidate Borda ranking, not the triplet, is the one to trust.

## 3. A profile coordinate system

In this concluding section of the chapter, let me be a bit more technical to explain the general story. Although symmetries are used to discover all flaws and inconsistencies of voting procedures for any number of candidates, they are awkward to use to construct and analyze examples. A more convenient approach is to use these symmetries to define a coordinate system in a profile space. Even better would be an orthogonal system; here, portions of a profile in a specified direction determine the behavior of a specified set of procedures over specified sets of candidates, but they have absolutely no influence on anything else.

This dream is realized for three candidates. But, while the orthogonality condition fails for more candidates, this is no serious trouble; using techniques that all mathematics graduate students learn early in their studies, there are standard ways to create the desired orthogonality.

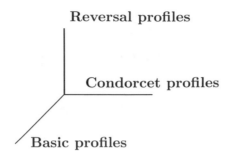

**Fig. 5.7** Profile coordinate system

**3.1. Three candidates.** For three candidates, Fig. 5.7 depicts the desired coordinate system in the five-dimensional space of profiles. The first coordinate directions (a two-dimensional system) consist of what I call *Basic profiles*. These profiles are a true delight in the sense that they experience absolutely no conflict; *all positional and pairwise procedures have the same ranking and even the same (normalized) tallies!* In an orthogonal direction are the *Condorcet* components which affect only the pairwise rankings. The final orthogonal direction (actually, two dimensional) consists of the *Reversal* components; these components have no effect on pairwise rankings, but they change the positional outcomes.

The approach starts with a neutral profile which has the same number of voters, $k$, for each strict ranking. Clearly, using $\mathbf{K}$ (for "kernel"), all positional and pairwise outcomes for

$$k\mathbf{K} = (k, k, k, k, k, k)$$

are ties. Rather than adding profiles to the starting $k\mathbf{K}$, voters are moved around. For instance, if five voters leave their original type-four preferences $(C \succ B \succ A)$ so that three of them now assume type-two preferences while the last three adopt type-six preferences, then the changes are given by $\mathbf{v} = (0, 3, 0, -5, 0, 2)$ and the new profile is $k\mathbf{K} + \mathbf{v}$.

So, a way to describe the different "profile coordinate directions" is to specify who changes preferences. Since only changes are being made, the sum of the components always equals zero. This reflects that all voters are still around; they just shifted beliefs. These "profile directions" are defined in an intuitive manner as follows.[12]

- The best news a candidate, say $A$, could have is that there had been an extreme shift in sentiment where voters who previously had $A$ bottom ranked now recognize her virtues and have her top ranked. There are only two ways to rank the candidates so that $A$ is bottom

---

[12]Remember, these artificial, highly concocted stories are intended only to provide intuition for mathematical terms. They do not describe what actually would happen.

ranked. So, as illustrated in Fig. 5.7a, the Basic profile, $\mathbf{B}_A$, has each of these voters leaving his previous attitude about $A$ to now have her top ranked.

As the tallies in Fig. 5.7a show, the change helps $A$ at the equal expense of the other two candidates. Also, the change in positional tallies (given by the values in parentheses) is independent of which $\mathbf{w}_s$ method is used. Namely, *all procedures agree with a profile constructed from Basic profiles.* Even the pairwise votes agree. This compatibility of pairwise and positional tallies shows that even when candidates are dropped, outcomes remain the same with a Basic profile. Basic profiles prohibit paradoxes.

- The Reversal portion of a profile reflects extreme attitudes. For an intuitive story, think of voters who are somewhat indifferent about $A$; they have her middle ranked. But a controversial TV interview with her affected the voters in opposite ways; half promoted $A$ to a top ranking while the other half demoted her to a bottom ranking. Since there are two ways to rank $A$ between $B$ and $C$, and since each of these choices leads to two changes in $A$'s ranking, the Reversal component for $A$, denoted by $\mathbf{R}_A$, involves four voters; there are two for each ranking where $A$ is middle ranked. As depicted in Fig. 5.7b, the voters from each ranking split; one now makes $A$ top ranked while the other makes her bottom ranked.

  As the tallies in the figure show, such a change enhances $A$'s standing for the plurality vote ($s = 0$) or any $s < \frac{1}{2}$, to the symmetric disadvantage of $B$ and $C$, it makes no difference whatsoever for the Borda Count ($s = \frac{1}{2}$), and it hurts $A$ to the symmetric advantage of $B$ and $C$ for the antiplurality vote ($s = 1$) and any $s > \frac{1}{2}$. No pairwise tallies are indicated because they all result in a zero-zero tie. Namely, the reversal terms do not effect the pairwise or Borda tallies.

- The Condorcet profile, denoted by $\mathbf{C}$, is where three voters defining a particular Condorcet triple move clockwise one ranking region to define the other Condorcet triple. The particular choice is depicted in Fig. 5.7c. This change affects only the pairwise tallies; each candidate gains a point in one pairwise contest but loses a point in the other one; this tally change also is in a clockwise manner.

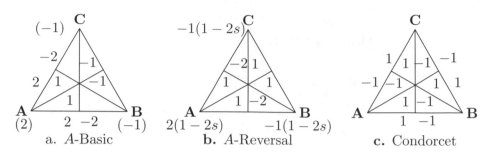

**Fig. 5.7.** Profile decomposition

By expressing these components as vectors, elementary computations prove that any Basic, Reversal, and Condorcet vector is pairwise orthogonal. The three Basic components, $\{\mathbf{B}_A, \mathbf{B}_B, \mathbf{B}_C\}$ are not orthogonal or even independent. Since addition proves that

$$(39) \qquad \mathbf{B}_C = -(\mathbf{B}_A + \mathbf{B}_B),$$

I usually use only $\mathbf{B}_A$ and $\mathbf{B}_B$. A similar symmetry story holds for the Reversal terms, that is,

$$(40) \qquad \mathbf{R}_C = -(\mathbf{R}_A + \mathbf{R}_B),$$

so I usually use only $\mathbf{R}_A$ and $\mathbf{R}_B$.

The above accounts for all profiles. This is because the Basic, Reversal, and Condorcet spaces are orthogonal, and the first two are two dimensional, so with $6k$ voters (from $k\mathbf{K}$), all five dimensions of the normalized simplex $\{\mathbf{p} = (p_1, \ldots, p_6) \mid \sum_{i=1}^{6} p_i = 6k\}$ are accounted for.

**3.2. Constructing examples.** The above description significantly simplifies the construction of examples which illustrate whatever is possible. All that is involved is to use the Fig. 5.7 tallies to design a desired behavior. After the coefficients in

$$(41) \qquad \mathbf{p} = a_B \mathbf{B}_A + b_B \mathbf{B}_B + a_R \mathbf{R}_A + b_R \mathbf{R}_B + \gamma \mathbf{C} + k\mathbf{K}$$

are determined, the desired profile is obtained by addition.

Suppose, for instance, we want an example where the Borda Count tally gives $A$ three more points than $B$, and $B$ six more points than $C$. According to the positional tallies of Fig. 5.7a, this goal is accomplished for all positional procedures with $6\mathbf{B}_A + 5\mathbf{B}_B + 3\mathbf{B}_C$. According to Eq. 39, this Basic profile component, $\mathbf{p}_{Basic}$, becomes

$$(42) \qquad \mathbf{p}_{Basic} = 6\mathbf{B}_A + 5\mathbf{B}_B - 3(\mathbf{B}_A + \mathbf{B}_B) = 3\mathbf{B}_A + 2\mathbf{B}_B.$$

To spice up the example, add an appropriate Condorcet component so that $B$ becomes the Condorcet winner. According to Fig. 5.7a, the $\mathbf{p}_{Basic}$ pairwise tallies have $A$ with 2 points and $B$ with $-2$ points. According to

Fig. 5.7c, a way to make $B$ the Condorcet winner is to add $-3\mathbf{C}$ to the mix leading to the partial profile component $(\mathbf{p}_{Basic} - 3\mathbf{C})$.

With $(\mathbf{p}_{Basic} - 3\mathbf{C})$, all positional rankings agree and have the same point spread between candidates. To create conflict with the positional outcomes, choose a positional method and a ranking. For simplicity, I select $s = -1$ and the antiplurality ranking of $C \succ B \succ A$. Creating an example with this behavior just requires using Fig. 5.7b to select appropriate reversal terms which do as desired. As $\mathbf{R}_A$ gives the antiplurality tallies to $A$, $B$, and $C$, respectively, of $-2, 1, 1$ points, it follows that $5\mathbf{R}_A + 3\mathbf{R}_B$ adds $5 \times (-2) + 3 \times 1 = -7$ points to $A$'s $\mathbf{p}_{Basic}$ antiplurality tally, $5 \times 1 + 3 \times (-2) = -1$ to $B$'s antiplurality tally, and $5 + 3 = 8$ to $C$'s tally to achieve the desired effect.

To convert this final expression into a true profile, there need to be enough starting voters so that no ranking has a negative number of voters. The ranking region which takes the hardest hit is the $C \succ A \succ B$ region where the entries add to $-12$. So, a profile with the desired effects is

$$\mathbf{p} = 3\mathbf{B}_A + 2\mathbf{B}_B - 3\mathbf{C} + 5\mathbf{R}_A + 3\mathbf{R}_B + 12\mathbf{K}.$$

**Some observations:**

The Eq. 41 coefficients need not be integers. For instance, to create a 25-voter example, the starting $k\mathbf{K}$ requires $6k$ voters, so we have $k = 4\frac{1}{6}$. Also, since $a_B\mathbf{B}_A + b_B\mathbf{B}_B$ gives $A$ a $3 \times (a_B - b_B)$ vote advantage over $B$, we would have to choose $a_B - b_B = \frac{1}{3}$, or have fractional coefficients, for $A$ to have a one-vote advantage over $B$. The only problem in using fractions is to ensure that the final profile has integer entries.

Some outcomes are impossible. For instance, if profile has the Borda ranking $A \succ B \succ C$ where $B$'s tally difference over $C$ is smaller than $A$'s over $B$, then it is impossible to construct an example where $B$ becomes the Condorcet winner. This is because the goal requires adding an appropriate multiple of the Condorcet term, $\mathbf{C}$, to change the $A \succ B$ Basic profile ranking. But because of the point spreads, this change reverses the $B \succ C$ pairwise ranking before it could affect the $A \succ C$ choice to create a cycle.

By using elementary algebra, a graph can be drawn to characterize all possible three-candidate election conflicts. Three-candidate graphs are in (Saari [**54**]), and abbreviated ones for more candidates are in (Saari [**56**, **57**]). These graphs illustrate facts such as the closer a positional method is to the Borda Count, the more unlikely it is to suffer certain election paradoxes.

**3.3. Finding procedures.** Remember the challenge of taking a given profile **p** and determining how different procedures would react. With the above Reversal and Condorcet components, it could meet the challenge if we knew **p**'s

(43)         $$\mathbf{p} = a_B \mathbf{B}_A + b_B \mathbf{B}_B + a_R \mathbf{R}_A + b_R \mathbf{R}_B + \gamma \mathbf{C} + k \mathbf{K}$$

decomposition.

This is not difficult to do. Expressing Eq. 43 in a matrix representation $\mathbf{p} = \mathcal{A}(\mathbf{v})$, matrix $T = \mathcal{A}^{-1}$ converts a standard profile **p** into its profile decomposition format.

(44)         $$T = \frac{1}{6} \begin{pmatrix} 2 & 1 & -1 & -2 & -1 & 1 \\ 1 & -1 & -2 & -1 & 1 & 2 \\ 0 & 1 & -1 & 0 & 1 & -1 \\ -1 & 1 & 0 & -1 & 1 & 0 \\ 1 & -1 & 1 & -1 & 1 & -1 \\ 1 & 1 & 1 & 1 & 1 & 1 \end{pmatrix}$$

What follows are examples of how $T(\mathbf{p})$ helps to explain the behavior of some profiles.

**3.4. Condorcet's example.** Recall, Fig. 5.3a represents Condorcet's historically important profile designed to discredit the Borda Count because it failed to elect the Condorcet winner. For a sharper description of this profile than permitted by the Fig. 5.3 analysis, with this $\mathbf{p} = (30, 1, 10, 1, 10, 29)$, the first two terms of $T(\mathbf{p}) = \frac{1}{6}(68, 76, -28, -20, 19, 81)$ require a $B \succ A \succ C$ Basic ranking. The next two terms (equivalent to $a_R = 0, b_R = \frac{8}{6}, c_R = \frac{28}{6}$) capture a Reversal effect favoring $B$ and $C$ which is so weak that it only changes the antiplurality ranking to $A \approx B \succ C$. The real impact is the $\gamma \mathbf{C}$ coefficient $\gamma = \frac{19}{6}$ and its strong cyclic distortion which changes the Condorcet winner from $B$ to $A$. As this cyclic effect reflects the loss of the assumption that the voters have transitive preferences, rather than supporting the Condorcet winner, this profile shows that Condorcet's procedure is susceptible to the distorting "ranking wheel" portion of a profile.

**3.5. Social Choice & Welfare election.** When the SC&W election was described on page 55, the procedure line and pairwise outcomes were used to suggest that $B$, not the actual winner $A$, better reflected the views of the voters. Now that we are armed with the profile decomposition, we can reexamine this assertion.

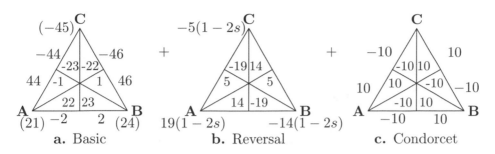

**Fig. 5.8.** SC&W Profile decomposition

As shown in Fig. 2.7, $\mathbf{p} = (13, 11, 0, 9, 8, 11)$ is the SC&W profile. The $T(\mathbf{p})$ outcome is displayed in Fig. 5.8. It is important to notice that each entry must be divided by six to reflect the $\frac{1}{6}$ multiple.

As the Basic (Fig. 5.8a) tallies show, the $B \succ A \succ C$ outcome was very close, by any measure, between the two top candidates. It is the fairly strong Reversal component, Fig. 5.8b, which defines the procedure line and allows $A$ to win with certain positional methods. Since the natural Approval Voting strategy in any closely contested election is to treat it as a plurality vote, this reversal term is what determined the actual election outcome.

An interesting effect is the fairly strong Condorcet term. The direction of this term assists $B$ over $A$; if it had been moving in the opposite direction, it would have made $A$, not $B$, the Condorcet winner.

**3.6. Unanimity profile.** Now consider the *unanimity profile* where all voters have the same $A \succ B \succ C$ preference. Intuition suggests that nothing surprising can occur, but this is not the case. The Basic terms of $T(\mathbf{p}) = \frac{1}{6}(2, 1, 0, -1, 1, 1)$ reproduce the $A \succ B \succ C$ ranking; somewhat unexpected are the Reversal and Condorcet terms. The Reversal terms[13] $a_R = c_R = \frac{1}{6}$ capture the conflict between plurality $A \succ B \sim C$ outcome and the unanimity $A \succ B \succ C$ preference. This difference is due to the fact that the plurality method fails Reversal symmetry; it has a component in the Reversal direction.

While the pairwise outcomes agree with the unanimity ranking, the tallies fail to reflect $A$'s distinct favored status. Indeed, the $\{A, B\}$, $\{B, C\}$, $\{A, C\}$ Basic pairwise outcomes of $(\frac{2}{6}, -\frac{2}{6})$, $(\frac{2}{6}, -\frac{2}{6})$, $(\frac{4}{6}, -\frac{4}{6})$ provide $A$ with a healthier spread over $C$ than over $B$. This diminished respect for $A$ in the usual pairwise election comes from the Condorcet coefficient $\gamma = \frac{1}{6}$ which introduces enough rotation in $C$'s favor to reduce $A$'s victory margin in their pairwise election. So, cyclic effects even influence unanimity outcomes; only the BC captures the essence of the unanimity profile.

---

[13]Obtained by using $\mathbf{R}_B = -(\mathbf{R}_A + \mathbf{R}_C)$.

# Chapter 6

# Other Procedures;
# Other Assumptions

A more appropriate title for this concluding chapter might be "potpourri," or maybe even "paella" as I will toss all of the leftovers into the stew. But, without a single theme, a brief outline is appropriate.

A good reason for studying voting methods is that they serve as a useful prototype for other aggregation methods. With all the problems which can arise in voting, we must wonder whether similar difficulties plague probability, statistics, economics, and the power indices used to describe the electoral college. This is the case, and a flavor of what can happen is described in Sect. 1.

Next I keep the promise made in the introductory chapter to indicate why there are 435 representatives in the U.S. House of Representatives. More than a footnote about American history, the discussion relates to all of those voting methods in Europe and South America called "proportional voting." A brief introduction to the mathematical structure is in Sect. 2.

Although voting problems and resolutions have been introduced, more remains to be discussed. The reason is that, as true with all research issues, a first take on the subject relies on simplifying assumptions. For instance, only positional and pairwise voting are described in the earlier chapters; can this material be used to analyze other methods such as Approval Voting and runoffs? (Yes.) Moreover, standard assumptions require the voters to rank all alternatives in a transitive manner. But anyone who has stood in a voting booth bewildered by the "judges" section of an overly long ballot has probably thought, "Who are these people?" So, it is not always true that all candidates can be ranked. Even more, some voters just plain refuse to follow instructions and vote for everyone. What can be done? An outline of how to tackle this topic is in Section 3.

## 1.   Beyond voting; other aggregation methods

It is interesting how all of those problems described in the first several chapters extend beyond voting to occur in probability, statistics, and many other areas. In fact, expect to encounter similar difficulties with any aggregation procedure. Not only are the problems and causes surprisingly similar, but so are resolutions. In other words, expect some version of the Chapter 5 "symmetry decomposition"[1] to hold for these other topics. To give a flavor of this, examples from probability, statistics, and power indices are used.

**1.1. Power indices.** My first example uses the power indices. Recall, these are the procedures used in the introductory chapter in order to examine the power of each state within the Electoral College.

Going far beyond the Electoral College, these indices are proving to be useful tools within the social sciences; e.g., they have been used to assign weights to the various countries when they cast ballots within the EU. These game theory tools have influenced U.S. Supreme Court decisions [**80**], they are used to understand interactions in the Economic Community (Berg [**7**], Brams [**12**], Nurmi and Meskanen [**35**]), the U.N. Security Council (Shapley and Shubik [**74**], Brams [**11**]), and the Canadian scheme for amending their Constitution (Miller [**30**], Straffin [**76**], Kilgour [**28**]). Other uses include analyzing the relative power of parties in a multiparty legislature, voting blocs in Congress, effects of voting groups in GATT, WTO, UN, NATO, and many other alphabetic arrangements which are intended to depict cooperative, political coalitions. (For references, see Shapley [**73**].) An early, intuitive use of these indices is the "small state – large state" controversy in the design of the U.S. Constitution; the compromise leading to two houses of Congress directly reflects the struggle to achieve parity in power.

While the more widely used power indices are those developed by Shapley and Banzhaf, other choices of the multipliers $\lambda_S$ have been proposed. To keep the argument relatively simple, I consider only those $\lambda$ weights which depend on the number of players in a coalition. But even in this restricted setting, a disturbing fact is that the power assigned to the different players can change with the choice of the indices. This feature has generated a large literature where the goal is to justify one choice of weights over another.

The problem is much worse; beyond giving different values, different indices *can define radically different rankings of the alternatives!* Namely,

---

[1]But, with different symmetries.

the power indices suffer the same kind of problems described in Chapter 2 for voting procedures. In this description, "profiles" are replaced with "games." Different games are described in terms of the payoff function $\nu$ in Eq. 1 which describes what different coalitions can attain.

**Theorem 13** (Saari and Sieberg [**62**]). *Suppose there are $N \geq 2$ players. For any $k$ satisfying $1 \leq k \leq N! - (N-1)!$, examples of the payoff function $\nu$ can be designed so that there are precisely $k$ different strict rankings of the $N$ players. The different rankings arise as the choice of the $\lambda_S$ weights change. It is impossible to find a game with more than $N! - (N-1)!$ strict power index rankings.*

*Once there are $N \geq 4$ players, there exist games where, with appropriate choices of the $\lambda_S$ multipliers, each player is listed in first, second, ..., and in last place.*

This result means, for instance, that there are games where the Shapley and Banzhaf values not only assign conflicting levels of power to different players, but the rankings can be directly opposite one another! So, what do these power indices really mean? As suggested with the voting problem, does a power index ranking reflect the contributions of the players, or the choice of the method? Because these procedures are widely used for pragmatic problems, the difference matters.

But if the same game allows many different power rankings, are we inviting strategic action? After the rewards for different coalitions are specified, could an appropriate strategic choice of the "power index" be made to try to persuade a "weak player" from complaining? In other words, can a power index be designed which makes it appear that this weak player has more power than actually is the case? Of course this can be done.

On the other hand, we also proved that no radical surprises occur with those special situations, as with the Electoral College, where the "power" of a coalition depends just on a vote count. Here, all methods give essentially the same ranking.

Incidentally, while the Shapley and Banzhaf rankings can differ as radically as desired, for this to happen there must be four or more players. This is because we also showed that certain indices must always rank the players in the same way. Surprisingly, these "invariant ranking" indices depend on the number of players rather than the kind of game. So, as the number of players changes, two indices which previously always shared the same ranking, now can differ as radically as desired.

The story about what happens when a player drops out remains at an early stage of research. After all, the issue was raised only recently [**62**], so we have not fully investigated what can, and cannot, happen. While we do know that dropping a player can cause havoc with the ranking of the remaining players, structural results remain to be discovered. In other words, while results showing that consistency in rankings cannot be expected when players drop out of the game, we have yet to find assertions ensuring some consistency in power rankings. They will come.

**1.2. Non-parametric statistics.** "Non-parametric statistics" is another subject area which, like positional voting, uses different weights to reach conclusions. The results given here were developed by Deanna Haunsperger [**22**]; some of the following examples come from an earlier paper (Haunsperger and Saari [**23**]).

As an example of these procedures, suppose data are collected to determine some measure of the life span of three machines. Since a longer lasting machine is preferred, assume that the measure is such that "more is better."

(45)

| Machine 1 | Machine 2 | Machine 3 |
|-----------|-----------|-----------|
| 5.89      | 5.81      | 5.80      |
| 5.98      | 5.90      | 5.99      |

The popular Kruskal-Wallis test (KW) ranks the machines by replacing the actual numbers in the table with ordinal rankings starting at the smallest. Then, the machines are ranked according to each machine's average ranking. Illustrating this approach with the Table 45 data, the individual rankings of

(46)

|       | Machine 1 | Machine 2 | Machine 3 |
|-------|-----------|-----------|-----------|
|       | 3         | 2         | 1         |
|       | 5         | 4         | 6         |
| **Total** | 8     | 6         | 7         |

define the KW ranking of

$$\text{Machine } 1 \succ \text{Machine } 2 \succ \text{Machine } 3.$$

The Kruskal-Wallis weights are only one choice among many possible possibilities. As Haunsperger shows, the choice of these different weights can generate all sorts of other rankings of the machines with the same data. In fact, she proves that data sets can be constructed which give conflicting outcomes similar to those described in the voting theorems in Chapter 2; e.g., the statistical ranking for the same data set can change with the ranking procedure.

But statistical methods are nonlinear procedures, so we should expect more of the "unexpected." As just a sampler of what else can happen, the following data defines a KW table identical to Table 46.

| | Machine 1 | Machine 2 | Machine 3 |
|---|---|---|---|
| (47) | 5.69 | 5.63 | 5.62 |
| | 5.74 | 5.71 | 6.00 |

It is somewhat surprising that even though each of the above "parts" (Tables 45 and 47) defines the same KW ranking, the combined data define the contrary KW ranking of

Machine 3 $\succ$ Machine 1 $\succ$ Machine 2.

Now turn to what can happen when alternatives are dropped. Voting, as we discovered in Chapter 3, can create a mess; the ranking after a candidate leaves may have nothing to do with the original ranking. The same behavior arises with these non-parametric methods. Haunsperger [22] proved that a result similar to Thm. 7 holds. The main change is to replace "voting methods" with "non-parametric statistical methods" and the "Borda Count" with the "Kruskal-Wallis test."

In part, she proves that the Kruskal-Wallis test admits all sorts of bothersome outcomes. For instance, even if an alternative appears to be "better than" any of the other choices (as determined by pairwise comparisons), it need not be at the top of the Kruskal-Wallis ranking. Stated in a simpler way, even though the pairwise comparisons suggest that Machine 2 is the best choice, because all pairwise rankings are consistent with

Machine 2 $\succ$ Machine 1 $\succ$ Machine 3,

the Kruskal-Wallis ranking could be

Machine 1 $\succ$ Machine 2 $\succ$ Machine 3.

A data set using the Kruskal-Wallis ranking numbers and exhibiting this behavior (Saari [52]) follows.

| Machine 1 | 4 | 5 | 9 | 12 | 13 | 17 | 21 | 22 | 26 |
|---|---|---|---|---|---|---|---|---|---|
| Machine 2 | 2 | 7 | 8 | 10 | 14 | 18 | 19 | 23 | 27 |
| Machine 3 | 1 | 3 | 6 | 11 | 15 | 16 | 20 | 24 | 25 |

While this conflict is not overly dramatic, trust me, I am trying to do my best. This is because while Haunsperger proved that the Kruskal-Wallis test admits all sorts of previously unexpected ranking inconsistencies when alternatives are dropped, she also showed that for non-parametric testing over $k$-samples, the Kruskal-Wallis test plays the role of the Borda Count in voting; it limits the kinds of paradoxes.

To summarize in overly simplified terms, Haunsperger's results can be described in two statements.

1. The Kruskal-Wallis test has problems, serious problems. All sorts of unexpected inconsistencies can occur as alternatives are dropped or added.

2. Among all of the non-parametric procedures of this type, the Kruskal-Wallis test is by far the best. No other procedure enjoys the level of consistency experienced by the Kruskal-Wallis test.

**1.3. Probability.** Assertions about probability are commonly illustrated with dice examples. Keeping with this tradition, let me indicate why we should expect different probability rankings when events are dropped.

Start with three dice which are fair in that any face is equally likely to occur with a roll. However, the faces on each die have unique numbers; each number appears twice. One possible choice is in Fig. 6.1.

As each die has three values, when two dice are used in a "high score wins" game, there are nine different possible outcomes; each is equally likely. Without the possibility of a tie (because each number appears on only one die), one of the two dice has to win at least 5 of the 9 possibilities. Since this die is more likely to win than the other, it is the "better" die.

With the Fig. 6.1 choices, it is clear that A is better than B, denoted as $A \succ B$. This is because the 11 on $A$ beats a 6, 8, or 10 on $B$, and the 9 on $A$ beats a 6 or 8 on $B$. Thus, $A$ wins five of the nine possible outcomes. Similarly, $B \succ C$ because both the 8 and 10 on the $B$ beat the 7 and 5 on the $C$, and the 6 on the $B$ beats the 5 on the $C$.

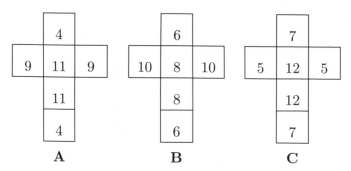

**Fig. 6.1.** Three dice

This information showing that these dice have the rankings

$$A \succ B, \quad B \succ C$$

suggests that $A \succ C$. This is not the case; instead, $C \succ A$ because $C$'s 12 beats $A$'s 4, 9, 11, and $C$'s 5 and 7 beat $A$'s 4. In other words, these three dice create a cycle.

The problem is much worse. As with Thm. 7, the result asserts that any desired behavior can happen. To be more general, replace "high score wins" with "high sum wins"; namely, roll a set of dice and then add the displayed numbers. If it is more likely for one set of dice to beat another, then it is the "better" choice.

To illustrate what can happen by staying with cycles, it is possible to create three sets of dice so that they form a cycle. Then, each of the large sets can be divided into three smaller sets of dice; these smaller sets also define cycles. The division process can continue. Or, rather than cycles, any desired choice of rankings between sets of dice, and then subsets of dice, and then ... can be imposed, and there exist choices of numbers to place on the faces of the dice so that a specified peculiarity will occur.

In other words, the full force of an assertion like Thm. 7 holds; rather than just voting, the theorem captures a general aggregation phenomenon. Indeed, Thm. 7 claims that there are threads of voting methods which allow consistency; similarly with this dice game, there is a restriction on the choice of assigned numbers to the dice which avoids all of these oddities. One central choice which plays a "Borda Count" role, of course, is to assign the same numbers to each die.

## 2. Apportioning congressional seats on a torus

"The presented numbers may not sum exactly to 100% due to rounding." How often have we encountered, and then dismissed, that traditional warning. Earlier, when discussing the 1860 presidential election, I reported a similar comment that was made about the data for each of the four candidates. We tend to ignore these warnings because the rounding off errors usually make little to no difference, that is, unless the errors can translate into a meaningful difference such as money or political power.

"Rounding off" difficulties become particularly important with an allocation of objects which cannot be split into parts. Examples where this may occur include a division of cars or cows among people, when determining how many people should be drafted into the army from each district, when computing the number of congressional seats to assign to each state according to census figures. Many European and South American countries use proportional voting schemes where the number of seats awarded to a party is based on the number of votes that were cast for the party.

To understand what can go wrong with all of these rounding off problems, let me describe a problem that can arise with the apportionment of Congressional seats to states according to census figures. To illustrate with small numbers, suppose there are only three states and nine seats in the House of Representatives. If one of the states has one-third of the total population, then it should receive three seats. But, what should happen if the House has ten seats? Since this state now is entitled to $3\frac{1}{3}$ seats, should this figure be rounded down to three, or up to four?

To explain the problems with census figures, Table 48 has the information about three states which are to apportion ten seats. Since State A has 43.3% of the population, it should have 43.3% of the seats, or 4.33. Using the same computations, the third column identifies the apportionments for all states. The point is that all of the states are entitled to a fractional number of seats, and all of the fractions are less than one-half.

In many situations of our daily life, it suffices to round numbers in the usual manner. For instance, with Table 48 where all fractions are less than a half, it might be tempting to round all of these numbers down to the nearest integer value. But, that approach fails here. The reason can be seen from the fourth column which shows that such a "rounding off" would assign only nine of the ten seats. Who should get the last one?

|         | % Pop. | Seats | Integer | Frac | Appor. |
|---------|--------|-------|---------|------|--------|
| State   |        |       |         |      |        |
| A       | 43.3   | 4.33  | 4       | 0.33 | 4      |
| B       | 42.3   | 4.23  | 4       | 0.23 | 4      |
| C       | 14.4   | 1.44  | 1       | 0.44 | 2      |
| **Total** | 100.0 | 10   | 9       | 1.00 | 10     |

(48)

Alexander Hamilton proposed that any extra seats should be assigned to the states according to size of the fractional parts of the exact apportionment. In our example, as $C$ has the largest fractional value of 0.44, it would be awarded the last remaining seat. The Hamilton apportionment is specified in the last column. Incidentally, a check of the 2000 apportionment proves that we do not use Hamilton's approach today. For instance, the exact 2000 apportionment for California is 52.447 while that for Utah is 3.457. Even though Utah has the larger fractional part, Utah's apportionment was rounded *down* to 3 while "representative rich" California had its apportionment rounded *up* to 53.[2]

While Hamilton's approach was used in the United States for decades, it ran into difficulties. To explain, recall that at an earlier time, the number of seats in the House could vary. To see what can happen with our example, the Hamilton apportionment for eleven seats is given next.

---

[2]This California – Utah anomaly is one of few interesting tidbits from the 2000 apportionment. The data, however, allows paradoxes for other procedures.

| State | % Pop. | Seats | Integer | Frac | Appor. |
|-------|--------|-------|---------|------|--------|
| $A$ | 43.3 | 4.763 | 4 | 0.763 | 5 |
| $B$ | 42.3 | 4.653 | 4 | 0.653 | 5 |
| $C$ | 14.4 | 1.584 | 1 | 0.584 | 1 |
| **Total** | 100.0 | 11 | 9 | 2.00 | 11 |

(49)

The point to notice is that with the same population figures and an increase in the House size, the smallest state, $C$, *loses* a representative. After each state is given the integer value of its exact apportionment, the total for the fourth column shows that two seats remain to be assigned. However, state $C$ now has the smallest fractional value, so these seats are assigned to $A$ and $B$.

This phenomenon is similar to an old story about three brothers dividing the inheritance of ten cows according to specified shares. The older brothers, $A$ and $B$, "kindly" decide to make the rewards more generous by jointly donating another cow. But by doing so, the younger brother, $C$, now gets one cow rather than two, and each of the older brothers gets an extra cow.

The mathematical source of the problem is obvious. With ten seats, state $A$ is entitled to $0.433 \times 10 = 4.33$ seats, while with eleven seats, the computation is $0.433 \times 11 = 0.433 \times (10 + 1) = 4.33 + 0.433$. In other words, a quick way to compute the new exact apportionment after a seat has been added is to add a state's decimal proportion to its previous exact apportionment. Of course, the larger states add a larger value to their total; this larger value allows their fractional portion of the apportionment to jump over that of the smaller states.

Just by playing with numbers and discovering how easy it is to create illustrating examples, one might suspect that this behavior occurs with a reasonable likelihood. This is the case (Saari [**39**]); with three or more groups (states, or whatever) involved in the division, almost all choices of the percentages for the different parties experience this phenomenon with some division size. Somewhat counterintuitive is the fact that the more accurate the census (so, the more terms in the decimal representation for each state), the more likely it is for this behavior to occur.

Not only is it likely for this behavior to occur, it has. In fact, in an attempt to select the House size to avoid this troublesome behavior, based on the 1910 census, the House size was set at 433 with one seat reserved for each of the two territories. In other words, it is this mathematical peculiarity which determined the current House size of 435.

While the history and mathematics of apportionments are fascinating topics, this current book is not the place to get into a lengthy discussion.

Instead, let me refer the interested reader to the fascinating results discovered by the Harvard mathematician E. Huntington [**25, 26**], the work of Balinski and Young [**3, 4**] which revived interest in this topic, and, for a mathematical description explaining why current "remedies" are far from being of much help, my book [**49**]. All that I wish to do here is to display a hidden mathematical property which ensures that this seemingly simple issue is mathematically delicate.

To keep the ideas simple, consider two parties, or states, or brothers, where $\mathbf{p} = (p_1, p_2)$ are the portions assigned to each group. Each $p_j$ is nonnegative and $p_1 + p_2 = 1$. Next, consider an initial allocation $\mathbf{a}(0) = (a_1, a_2)$; these $a_i$ values might be the assignment of one seat per state before using population figures, it might be that each party starts with zero seats and the percentage figures determine all, it might be that each state is entitled to a certain initial allocation of money for seniors.

The exact allocation is given by adding $t\mathbf{p} = t(p_1, p_2)$ to the starting allocation where $t$ is an integer. For instance, if state 1 is entitled to $\frac{6}{7}$ of any extras, and state 2 to $\frac{1}{7}$, then with one extra item the division is $1(\frac{6}{7}, \frac{1}{7}) = (\frac{6}{7}, \frac{1}{7})$. With 15 extra items, the extra division is $15(\frac{6}{7}, \frac{1}{7}) = (12\frac{6}{7}, 2\frac{1}{7})$

These numbers are placed at fixed distances along the exact apportionment line

$$(50) \qquad \mathbf{a}(t) = \mathbf{a}(0) + t\mathbf{p} = (a_1 + tp_1, a_2 + tp_2).$$

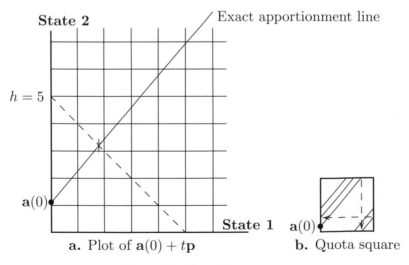

**Fig. 6.2.** Hamilton's scheme

Hamilton's allocation scheme can be represented by plotting the Eq. 50 *exact apportionment line* on graph paper as illustrated in Fig. 6.2a; this is the solid line moving toward the north-east. The actual amounts to distribute are given by points along this line; e.g., the dagger represents one such point with a total of five seats. The vertical and horizontal grid lines identify, respectively, different integer assignments to States 1 and 2. With $h = 5$ seats to distribute, the dashed line indicates all choices for the two states that add to 5. The apportionment line does not cross the dashed line at an integer. But, the closest integer point (on the dashed line) to this crossing point with a dagger is $(2, 3)$. Therefore, the Hamilton apportionment is two units to State 1 and three to State 2.

As we discovered from Tables 48 and 49, only a state's fractional part matters. So, maybe only these fractional terms should be plotted. Each square designates different integer values for the states, so the points on the line in a square are the fractional values. To plot these fractional values, cut out the squares which contain a portion of the apportionment line, and then stack them. This creates Fig. 6.2b where, for convenience, the squares are magnified.

When cutting a square, if the apportionment line hits a top edge, as true with the first square, then the line starts at the bottom edge of the next square at an equal distance to the right. Thus, when these two squares are stacked, the bottom edge point is directly below the top one; the vertical arrow in Fig. 6.2b shows this for the first and second squares. Similarly, if the apportionment line leaves the right edge of a square, then it enters the left edge of the next square at the same height; when these two squares are stacked, these right and left points are at the same height. The horizontal arrow in Fig. 6.2b captures this behavior for the second and third squares. Figure 6.2b displays the stacking of the first five squares of Fig. 6.2a.

Now notice that the two horizontal edges of our square represent where State 2's apportionment has a zero fractional part. So, as indicated in Fig. 6.3a, glue these two edges together to create the cylinder of Fig. 6.3b. This gluing reconnects all of the Fig. 6.2b line segments which were split when hitting a top edge of a square.

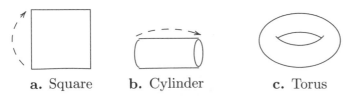

**a.** Square        **b.** Cylinder        **c.** Torus

**Fig. 6.3.** Making a torus from a square

Next, connect what were the square's two side edges; as indicated by the arrow in Fig. 6.3b, this means that the ends of the Fig. 6.3b cylinder are glued together. The result is the Fig. 6.3c object which resembles the surface of a donut; it is called a torus and it is denoted by $T^2$ where the "2" represents the dimension. The gluing connects the disconnected lines of Fig. 6.2b to make it continuous again. So, this line, which captures the nature of the fractional part of the apportionments, winds around the torus.

The same construction holds for any number of states. For three states, the square is replaced with a cube. Connecting opposite faces creates a three-dimensional torus $T^3$. Don't try to do this at home because the construction requires living in a four-dimensional world. While this cube construction is an out-of-our-world experience, remember that the apportionment problems for the 50 states of the U.S. are subject to the mathematical structure of a fifty-dimensional torus, $T^{50}$.

The punch line that I am heading toward concerns an interpretation of that line drawn on the torus. Remember, the exact apportionments are points—given by integer values of $t$—which are spaced equal distances along this line. When expressed in terms of dynamics, these points represent chaotic dynamics. Indeed, one of the simplest forms of "chaotic dynamics" can be constructed with this spacing of points on a line wrapping around a torus coming from the exact apportionment line of Fig. 6.1a with an irrational slope. In this setting, the line never ends; it keeps winding around the torus until it comes close to filling all the space. In fact, these equally spaced points come arbitrarily close to any point on the torus.

Now, apportionment problems do not permit irrational slopes. But the sharper the population figures, the more terms in the decimal representations of the populations, and the closer the figures are to irrationals. In turn, the line — and the specific exact apportionments — come close to filling the torus. Hence the fractional part has to enter any region which unleashes a "paradox."

The real difficulty with apportionment problems, then, is that the hidden chaotic effects allow the apportionment values to jump into unexpected regions. For this reason, whatever method we invent, expect problems. In fact, some of these problems are so severe that, with a fixed House size, I believe we should return to Hamilton's method.

## 3. Other procedures, and other assumptions

The symmetry structure introduced in the last chapter resolved many of the puzzles of voting methods. But the discussion was limited to positional and pairwise voting. What about other voting methods, such as Approval Voting, and what about realistic concerns such as when voters cannot rank everyone or have ties in their preferences?

The approach is essentially the same. First, find the underlying symmetry structure of the newly posed problem, and then find settings that should lead to ties. While this is the approach, to keep my comments brief, different arguments are given to support the following ways to get around these problems.

**3.1. Runoffs.** With only minimal effort, the decomposition approach developed in the last chapter can be used to analyze a wide selection of voting methods. In describing what to do, my emphasis will be on two kinds of procedures: those which involve different subsets of candidates and those which involve different procedures for the same set of candidates.

A runoff election is a typical election procedure which involves different subsets of candidates. The first election usually is a plurality vote of all candidates and the second election is a majority vote, pairwise comparison of the two top-ranked candidates.

To illustrate a use of the decomposition, suppose we wish to create an example where it is debatable whether the correct candidate wins with an Instant Runoff Procedure. This is easy; select the Basic terms so that the outcome is $A \succ B \succ C$. Now, choose the Reversal terms so that the plurality outcome is $C \succ B \succ A$; this means that because of the plurality procedure's inability to recognize the cancelling effect of the Reversal symmetry, $A$ becomes bottom ranked — and is dropped. The profile as it stands, has pairwise rankings consistent with $A \succ B \succ C$ so $B$ will be the winner. However, it is possible to add a Condorcet effect so that $A$ remains the Condorcet winner but $C$ beats $B$ in the pairwise tallies. So, by several measures, this procedure drops the superior candidate.

**3.2. From truncated ballots to Approval Voting.** A large class of procedures uses different positional methods with the same set of candidates. "Truncated voting" is where a voter refuses to vote for all candidates. In a Borda election, for instance, if voters are permitted to vote for only one of the three candidates, then the voters can select between using $(2, 1, 0)$ or $(2, 0, 0)$ as the tallying method. With cumulative voting where, say, two votes are given to a voter and they can be split in any desired manner, the voter selects either $(2, 0, 0)$ or $(1, 1, 0)$ to tally his or her ballot. As Approval Voting allows a voter to vote for one, or for two candidates, the voter is choosing to have the ballot tallied with $(1, 0, 0)$ or $(1, 1, 0)$.

A simple way to analyze these procedures is to split the voters into the groups that use each of the choices, analyze what happens with each group, and then add the effects. Let me illustrate with AV by again using the Social Choice & Welfare election.

For AV, divide the voters into the "plurality" (those who voted for one candidate) and the "antiplurality" (those who voted for two candidates) groups. As the data [**14**] for this election had only one voter voting for two candidates, this voter with preferences $A \succ B \succ C$ defines the "antiplurality group." The plurality group consists of the remaining 51 voters.

Each group's profile decomposition is in Table 51 where the plurality voters are the first block. Namely, the Reversal tallies for the first block use the plurality vote, while those for the second block of antiplurality voters have antiplurality Reversal tallies. Remember, all terms are to be divided by 6.

|  | $A$ | $B$ | $C$ | $A$ | $B$ | $C$ |
|---|---|---|---|---|---|---|
| **Basic** | 18 | 24 | $-42$ | 3 | 0 | $-3$ |
| **Reversal** | 18 | $-12$ | $-6$ | $-1$ | 2 | $-1$ |
| **Subtotals** | 36 | 12 | $-48$ | 2 | 2 | $-4$ |
| **Total** | 38 | 14 | $-52$ | | | |

(51)

The Table 51 tallies prove (as common sense suggests) that the larger "plurality" group dominates the AV outcome. Their $B \succ A \succ C$ Basic tallies, $\frac{24}{6} = 4$, 3, and $-7$, demonstrate the closeness — a single vote differential — of the $A$, $B$ election. What forces the AV conflicting conclusion is the procedure's reliance on the stronger $A \succ B \succ C$ Reversal values of $\frac{18}{6} = 3$, $-2$, and $-1$. In other words, the distorting Reversal term, which has no effect on pairwise and BC behavior, ensure $A$'s AV victory; the "antiplurality group" adds nothing to this competition.

Incidentally, this decomposition demonstrates why, contrary to claims of some of the AV supporters, when the AV elects the Condorcet winner, this must be treated as a pure coincidence rather than an AV election effect. This is because beyond the Basic terms, the Approval Voting conclusion is totally governed by Reversal terms which have no effect on pairwise outcomes, while the Condorcet winner is influenced by Condorcet effects which have no influence on the AV ranking.

**3.3. Who are these guys?** Voting theory would be much easier if voters behaved according to the assumptions made by the theorists. But this need not happen. I, along with many other people, cannot always rank all of the candidates. At other times, I do not have a strict ranking; for instance, after a recent debate, I might rank Darlene first, Mavis and Bobbie tied for second, and Lorraine last. How should these settings be handled?

Actually, these situations can be addressed in much the same way as above. The main difference is that new assumptions about voter preferences introduce new symmetries. In turn, there are new arrangements of voters' preferences which should define a tied ballot. For instance, if three voters have the preferences $A \succ B \approx C$, $B \succ C \approx A$, and $C \succ A \approx B$, it is difficult to find an advantage for any candidate, so a tie should result.

Rather than going through all of the details, let me provide a quick sense of one way to handle this. First, notice that the tallies for the Borda Count are intimately related to pairwise tallies.

To see this arrangement, suppose a voter has preferences $A \succ B \succ C$. The Borda Count would assign 2, 1, and 0 points, respectively, to $A$, $B$, and $C$. Now consider the number of points this voter would assign to the three candidates over the three pairwise elections.

(52)

| Pairs | $A$ | $B$ | $C$ |
|---|---|---|---|
| $\{A, B\}$ | 1 | 0 | |
| $\{A, C\}$ | 1 | | 0 |
| $\{B, C\}$ | | 1 | 0 |
| **Total** | 2 | 1 | 0 |

In other words, the Borda Count is a natural extension of the pairwise vote in the sense that it assigns a candidate the same number of points a voter would cast for her over the pairwise elections. The same interpretation for the Borda Count holds for any number of candidates.

Now suppose a voter can only determine his favorite, or maybe, he really doesn't care about the others; his preferences are $A \succ (B \approx C)$. To score such preferences, suppose that, in a pairwise vote, the voter has one point to split. In this setting, the voter casts the following points for each candidate.

(53)

| Pairs | $A$ | $B$ | $C$ |
|---|---|---|---|
| $\{A, B\}$ | 1 | 0 | |
| $\{A, C\}$ | 1 | | 0 |
| $\{B, C\}$ | | $\frac{1}{2}$ | $\frac{1}{2}$ |
| **Total** | 2 | $\frac{1}{2}$ | $\frac{1}{2}$ |

These values suggest that a natural modification of the Borda Count is to change the $(2, 1, 0)$ scoring by averaging the points assigned to the tie votes. While it is not obvious, this approach minimizes the number and kinds of inconsistencies which can occur when ties are allowed. Of course, an equivalent approach is to use $(\frac{3}{2}, 0, 0)$.[3] A similar approach provides answers when there are more candidates, when there are ties, when the voters have only a partial ranking, and so forth.

---

[3]In other words, a voter has an incentive to vote for only one candidate to give the candidate a boost. A simple way to minimize this strategic action is to interpret the BC as giving a point differential for each candidate. Thus, a truncated ballot assigns only one point to the candidate.

## 4.  Concluding comment

One of the main messages of this book is, *"Beware!"* Beware of aggregation procedures because, in an unexpected manner, they allow unanticipated behavior. This is particularly troubling with voting. Without understanding what can happen in elections, we run the very real risk of choosing badly. And a bad election decision is not something that is with us only for a short time; it is something which can shape the direction of a social group, department, state, or even the country. When possible, we must make wise decisions.

# Bibliography

[1] Adams, W. H., *The Paris Years of Thomas Jefferson*, Yale University Press, New Haven, 1997.

[2] Arrow, K.J. *Social Choice and Individual Values*, 2nd ed., Wiley, New York, 1963.

[3] Balinski, M., and H.P. Young, The quota method of apportionment, *Amer. Math. Monthly* **82** (1975), 701-730.

[4] Balinski, M., and H.P. Young, *Fair Representation*, Yale University Press, New Haven, 1982.

[5] Banzhaf, J., 1965, Weighted voting doesn't work; a mathematical analysis. *Rutger's Law Review* **19**, 317-343.

[6] Banzhaf, J., 1966, Multi-member electoral districts; Do they violate the one man, one vote principle? *Yale Law Journal* **75**, 1309-1338.

[7] Berg, S. 1999, On voting power indices and a class of probability distributions: with applications to EU data, *Group Decision and Negotiation* **8** 17-31.

[8] Black, D., *The Theory of Committees and Elections*, Cambridge University Press, London, 1958.

[9] Bliss, G., Brown, E.W., Eisenhart, L.P, and Pearl, R., *Report to the President of the Nat. Acad. Sci.* , 1929.

[10] Borda, J. C., *Mémoire sur les élections au scrutin*. Histoire de l'Académie Royale des Sciences, Paris, 1781.

[11] Brams, S. *Rational Politics*, Congressional Quarterly Inc., Washington DC, 1985.

[12] Brams. S., *Negotiation Games*, Routledge, London 1990.

[13] Brams, S., and P. Fishburn, *Approval Voting*, Birkhauser, Boston, 1982.

[14] Brams, S., and P. Fishburn, A nail biting election, To appear in *Social Choice & Welfare*.

[15] Brams, S., P. Fishburn, S. Merrill, The responsiveness of approval voting: Comments on Saari and Van Newenhizen, *Public Choice* **59** (1988), 2112-131.

[16] Condorcet, M., *Éssai sur l'application de l'analyse à la probabilité des décisions rendues à la pluralité des voix*. Paris, 1785.

[17] Coxeter, H.S.M., The functions of Schläfli and Lobatschefsky, Quarterly Journal of Mathematics, **6** (1935), 13-29.

[18] Deegan, J. and W. Packel, 1978, A new index of power for simple n-person games, *International Journal of Game Theory* **7**, 113-123.

[19] Gibbard, A., Manipulation of Voting Schemes: a general result, *Econometrica* **41** (1973), 587-601.

[20] Gillman, L., Approval voting and the coming MAA elections, *Focus,* March-April, 1098.

[21] Guinier, L., *The Tyranny of the Majority,* Macmillan, Inc., New York, 1994.

[22] Haunsperger, D., Dictionaries of paradoxes for statistical tests on $k$-samples, *Jour. Amer. Statistical Assoc.* **87** (1992), 249-272.

[23] Haunsperger, D., and D. G. Saari, The lack of consistency for statistical decision procedures, *American Statistician* **45** (1991), 252-255.

[24] Herold, J. C., *The Age of Napoleon,* Houghton Mifflin, Boston, 1963.

[25] Huntington, E., The mathematical theory of the apportionment of representatives, *Proceedings of the National Academy of Sciences* **7** (1921), 123-127.

[26] Huntington, E., The apportionment of representatives in Congress, *Trans. American Math. Society* **30** (1928), 85-110.

[27] Kelly, J., *Arrow Impossibility Theorems,* Academic Press, New York, 1978.

[28] Kilgour, D.M., 1983, A formal analysis of the amending formula of Canada's Constitution Act, 1982, *Canadian Journal of Political Science,* **16**, 771-777.

[29] Merlin, V. and D. G. Saari, Copeland method II: manipulation, monotonicity, and paradoxes, *Journal of Economic Theory* **72** (1997), 148-172.

[30] Miller, D, 1973, A Shapley value analysis of the proposed Canadian constitutional amendment scheme, *Canadian Journal of Political Science,* **4**, 140-143.

[31] McLean, I., The first golden age of social choice, 1783-1803, in *Social Choice, Welfare, and Ethics,* eds. Barnett, W., Moulin, H., Salles, M., and N. Schofield, Cambridge University Press, 1995.

[32] McLean, I., and F. Hewitt, *Condorcet: Foundations of Social Choice and Political Theory,* Edward Elgar, 1994.

[33] Nanson, E.J., *Methods of election,* Trans. Proc. Roy. Society Victoria **18** (1882), 197-240.

[34] Nurmi, H., *Voting Paradoxes and How to Deal with Them,* Springer-Verlag, NY, 1999.

[35] Nurmi, H., and T. Meskanen, 1999, A priori power measures and the institutions of the European Union, *European Journal of Political Research* **35** 161-179.

[36] Ordeshook, P.C., *Game theory and political theory,* Cambridge University Press, New York, 1986.

[37] Paulos, J., Commentary on the ABC news web page, Nov. 13, 2000.

[38] Riker, W. H., *Liberalism against Popularism: A Confrontation between the Theory of Democracy and the Theory of Social Choice,* Freeman, San Francisco, CA, 1982.

[39] Saari, D. G. Methods of apportionment and the House of Representatives, *American Mathematical Monthly* **85** (1978), 792-802.

[40] Saari, D. G., The ultimate of chaos resulting from weighted voting systems, *Advances in Applied Mathematics* **5** (1984), 286–308.

[41] Saari, D. G., A dictionary for voting paradoxes, *Journal of Economic Theory* **48** (1989), 443-475.

[42] Saari, D. G., Susceptibility to manipulation, *Public Choice* **64** (1990), 21-41.

[43] Saari, D. G., The Borda Dictionary, *Social Choice and Welfare* **7** (1990), 279-317.

[44] Saari, D. G., Calculus and extensions of Arrow's Theorem, *Journal of Mathematical Economics* **20** (1991), 271-306.

[45] Saari, D. G., Symmetry extensions of "neutrality" I. Advantage to the Condorcet loser. *Soc. Choice & Welfare* **9** (1992), 307-336.

[46] Saari, D. G., Millions of election rankings from a single profile, *Soc. Choice & Welfare* **9** (1992), 277-306.

[47] Saari, D. G., The aggregate excess demand function and other aggregation procedures. *Economic Theory* **2** (1992), 359-388.

[48] Saari, D. G., *Geometry of Voting*, Springer-Verlag, New York, 1994.

[49] Saari, D. G., *Basic Geometry of Voting*, Springer-Verlag, New York, 1995.

[50] Saari, D. G., A chaotic exploration of aggregation paradoxes, *SIAM Review* **37** (1995), 37-52.

[51] Saari, D. G., The mathematical complexity of simple economics, *Notices of the American Mathematical Society* **42** (1995), No. 2: 222-230.

[52] Saari, D. G., Nonparametric tests: paradoxes, in *Encyclopedia of Statistical Sciences*, Update Vol. 2. ed. Kotz, S., Read, C., Banks, D., 485-489, John Wiley & Sons, 1998.

[53] Saari, D. G., Connecting and resolving Sen's and Arrow's Theorems, *Social Choice & Welfare* **15** (1998), 239-261.

[54] Saari, D. G., Explaining all three-alternative voting outcomes, *Journal of Economic Theory* **87** (1999), 313-335.

[55] Saari, D. G., More chaos, but in voting and apportionments? *Proceedings of the National Academy of Sciences* **96** (Sept. 14, 1999), 10568-10571.

[56] Saari, D. G., Mathematical structure of voting paradoxes I: pairwise vote, *Economic Theory* **15** (2000), 1-53.

[57] Saari, D. G., Mathematical structure of voting paradoxes II: positional voting, *Economic Theory* **15** (2000), 55-101.

[58] Saari, D. G., Suppose you want to vote strategically, *Math Horizons* (Nov. 2000), 5-10.

[59] Saari, D. G., Analyzing a nail-biting election, to appear, *Social Choice & Welfare*.

[60] Saari, D. G., *Decisions and Elections; Explaining the Unexpected*, Cambridge University Press, in press.

[61] Saari, D. G., and V. Merlin, Changes that cause changes, *Social Choice & Welfare*, August 2000.

[62] Saari, D. G., and K. K. Sieberg, Some surprising properties of power indices, *Games and Economic Behavior*, 2001.

[63] Saari, D. G., and K. K. Sieberg, The sum of the parts can violate the whole, NU Preprint, 1999.

[64] Saari, D. G., and M. Tataru, The likelihood of dubious election outcomes, *Economic Theory* **13** (1999), 345-363.

[65] Saari, D. G., and F. Valognes, The geometry of Black's single peakedness and related conditions. *Journal of Mathematical Economics* **32** (1999), 429-456.

[66] Saari, D. G., and J. Van Newenhizen, The problem of indeterminacy in approval, multiple, and truncated voting systems, *Public Choice* **59** (1988), 101–120.

[67] Saari, D. G., and J. Van Newenhizen, Is approval voting an "unmitigated evil," *Public Choice* **59** (1988), 133–147.

[68] Satterthwaite, M., Strategyproofness and Arrow's conditions, *Journal of Economic Theory* **10** (1975), 187-217.

[69] Schläfli, L., Theorie der vielfachen Kontinuität, Gesammelte Mathematische Abhandlungen. Basel: Birkhauser 1950.

[70] Sen, A., A possibility theorem on majority decisions, *Econometrica* **34** (1966), 491-499.

[71] Shapley, L. S. A value for n-person games, in *Contributions to the Theory of Games II,* ed., H.W. Kuhn and A. W. Tucker, Annals of Mathematics Studies **28** (1953), 307-317.

[72] Shapley, L. S., Valuation of games, pp 55-68 in *Game Theory and its Applications,* ed. W. Lucas, AMS, Providence RI, 1981.

[73] Shapley, L. S. Measurement of power in political systems, pp 69-81 in *Game Theory and its Applications,* ed. W. Lucas, AMS, Providence RI, 1981.

[74] Shapely, L. and M. Shubik, A method for evaluating the distribution of power in a committee system, *American Political Science Review* **48** (1954), 787-792.

[75] Sieberg, K., *Criminal Dilemmas,* Springer-Verlag, New York, 2001.

[76] Straffin, P., Homogeneity, independence and power indices, *Public Choice* **30** (1977), 107-118.

[77] Straffin, P., Power and stability in politics, pp. 1128-1151 in *Handbook of Game Theory, Vol. 2,* ed. R. Aumann, S. Hart, Elsevier Science, Amsterdam, 1994.

[78] Tabarrok, A., Fundamentals of voting theory illustrated with the 1992 election, or could Perot have won in 1992? Ball State University preprint, 3/6/97; to appear in *Public Choice.*

[79] Tabarrok, A., and L. Spector, Would the Borda Count have avoided the civil war? *Journal of Theoretical Politics* **11** (1999), 261-288.

[80] U.S. Supreme Court, *Whitcomb vs. Chavis* 400 US 143, 1970.

# Index